PICUS WHO IS ALSO ZEUS

T0370850

PICUS WHO IS ALSO ZEUS

by

RENDEL HARRIS

Cambridge :
at the University Press
1916

CAMBRIDGE
UNIVERSITY PRESS

University Printing House, Cambridge CB2 8BS, United Kingdom

Cambridge University Press is part of the University of Cambridge.

It furthers the University's mission by disseminating knowledge in the pursuit of education, learning and research at the highest international levels of excellence.

www.cambridge.org
Information on this title: www.cambridge.org/9781316509531

First published 1916
First paperback edition 2015

A catalogue record for this publication is available from the British Library

ISBN 978-1-316-50953-1 Paperback

INTRODUCTION

THE present volume is a continuation of the one which was published in 1913 under the title of *Boanerges*, much in the same way as *Boanerges* was the expansion and extension of the previous volumes dealing with the *Dioscuri in Christian Legend*, and the *Cult of the Heavenly Twins*, which are cited in the following pages under the abbreviated forms, *Dioscuri* and *Cult* respectively. It is assumed (for how could one continue the argument on any other hypothesis?) that the main positions in the previous volume are sound, and that they furnish a secure foundation upon which the students of Man and of Man's Religions may build further: this does not mean that there are no corrections necessary and no re-statements desirable, but that, on the whole, we have liberty to proceed: for the investigation, as far as it has gone, has thrown too much light into odd corners of human history to be altogether negligible. The student of classical archaeology cannot afford to ignore it, for it explains many hitherto unintelligible features in Greek and Roman Mythology, and shows us in what direction to look for the origin of the Olympian worship. The student of history cannot pass by discoveries which, to a large extent, enable us to re-write the story of the foundation of Rome and other great cities of the past. Folk-lore, folk-medicine, and the like, begin to be translated out of a thousand languages into a single speech, expressing the Unity of Civilisation and the Interrelation of Religions. Let us see how far we have gone, and then we shall see the lines that are laid for the progress of the present volume.

It has been shown that mankind, in its primitive state, the subject of many fears, and evolving its faith from its fears ("*primus in orbe deos fecit timor*"), found itself beset especially by two Fears, one the great rational Fear, the Fear of the Thunder, the other, the great irrational Fear, the Fear of Twin Children. From the first of these Fears came the worship of Zeus, from the second the reverence for the children of the Thunder, known by various names as Dioscuri, Boanerges, and the like. The road to Zeus-worship was shown to start from the belief that the Thunder was a bird, and commonly the explanation was made that it was a bird with a red head. In particular the bird which personified the Thunder over Europe and part of Asia (and perhaps elsewhere) was the Red-headed Woodpecker, omitting for convenience some associated bird-forms that have slight claims to similar rank. This Red-headed Woodpecker, either the Great Black Woodpecker, the *Picus Martius* of ancient Latins and of the modern Zoologists, or the Green Woodpecker, the *Gecinus Viridis*, dominates the whole religious evolution of Greece and Rome. He is the "Picus who is also Zeus" of the Cretan and Italian tradition, the good King Keleos (sometimes the bad Keleos) of Cretan and Eleusinian story. From one or other of these forms the Zeus and the Jupiter with which we are familiar have been derived; and the colour with which he is supposed to symbolise the thunder becomes a religious token of the first moment, in Europe, Asia and Africa, as well among the priesthood of the Capitoline Jupiter as among the soldiery of the Spartans, and the medicine-men of tribes of West Africa. It was pointed out also that this Thunder-god who was a bird and became a man made his evolution in easy stages, and that we could catch him in the transition from the ornithomorph to the anthropomorph, among existing people like the American Indians of the Pacific slope, who confess him in both forms, or among the Chinese and Japanese who figure him, indeed, as a man, but encumber the human form with bird-like appendages, in the shape of claws and wings and a beak-like nose, in order that we may say in Chinese the equivalent of the Cretan formula that "Picus is also Zeus." Something of the same kind may, perhaps, be traced in the early Vedic religion.

When we came to the second great primal Fear, we were able to show it to be diffused over almost the whole world, and frequently to be expressed in what we could only describe at the present day as acts of systematic and revolting cruelty. It appears that primitive man was in the habit of making away with any woman who bore twins, and that the twin-children were themselves destroyed; sometimes reason came to the relief of the situation and sometimes humanity asserted itself: in such cases it was argued that only one child was abnormal, it was a spirit-child, a devil-child, a bird-child, a thunder-child, and therefore only one was killed. The theory of a dual paternity changed the situation, exile was substituted for murder, and the Twin-village was formed; we thus discovered one of the missing origins of human Sanctuary, in the island or bush-clearing, where the exiled twins and their mother were allowed to live, but under the severest of taboos. Moreover since, in many parts of the world, the supposition that the second parent in the fatherhood of a pair of twins was regarded as a bird, and particularly as the bird which was the thunder, there was a blending of the two great Fears into a single and combined Reverence, in which the Thunder and the Twins were a sacred triad, known to the Greeks as Zeus and the Dioscuri (or Zeus' boys), and revered in common; similar evolutions occurred elsewhere, and even religions that became monotheistic, like the Hebrew religion, for a long time did not regard it as impious or idolatrous to associate a pair of celestial Sons of Thunder with the central worship of Jahveh.

Probably the discovery that will be most far-reaching in connection with Twins and the Thunder-cult is precisely that of the Twin-town. We can already begin to mark the twin-towns upon our classical maps, just as we can do in the Niger district, and, as we hope to show in the present volume, on the map of England.

It is not, of course, maintained that one can, all over the world, find Thunder-cults, either in the present or the past; nor that the Twin-Fear is universal; nor that the areas of the one Fear are necessarily the areas of the other, so that every Thunder-bird would have Thunder-children, and there would be a pair of Dioscures for every sacred Woodpecker. It is not necessary to assume that there was a Thunder-bird in ancient Egypt, where there is not normally any Thunder; we may not always be able to connect the Twin-cult with the Thunder-cult, even where both of them exist. All that we at present assert is that in the course of human evolution the two fears in question have existed over very wide areas, and that the areas where they do exist overlap one another widely. That will be a sufficient statement from which to work.

In the region of Greek Mythology, our gains have been very great. The legends of the birth of Zeus are now reasonably intelligible. The Curetes and Corybantes who protect with their clatter and clamour the infant god turn out to be the counterpart of the humble peasantry who call the swarming bees by beating upon tin pans! And the reason why the bee-maidens and others fed the babe Zeus with honey arises out of a very natural supposition that the Woodpecker, who is the Thunder-bird and is also Zeus, has a fondness for bees and bee-products. We ought, of course, to have found out long ago the riddle of the Curetes and Corybantes, for it was disclosed in unambiguous language by Vergil himself.

The Heavenly Twins were shown to be the patrons of many human arts and industries, especially they were credited with the invention of the Plough and the invention of the Ship. It was shown that in each case the Woodpecker parent was really responsible. From this point a new departure was made with the greatest of all the Greek Myths, the story of the Argonauts. Jason was shown to be a Heavenly Twin and his ship to be manned, for the most part, by pairs of twin heroes. The ship had been evolved out of a dug-out with twins on board, just such an *alveus* as Romulus and Remus were exposed in on the Tiber!

The religious importance of the enquiries became clear when the results were applied to the Christian Scriptures. In the Old Testament and in the Apocrypha there were shown to be many stories that were based upon twin-myths, and it was evident that such beliefs in twin-myths lasted nearly to the borders of the Christian era, so far as literary evidence was forthcoming. Perhaps the best instances will be found in the explanations that were made of the story of Esau and Jacob, the inverted birthright in these legends being capable of immediate illustrations from West African twin-customs.

If literary evidence for Dioscurism was in evidence down to the borders of the Christian era, it goes without saying that the Twins were current in folk-lore in the times of the N.T. itself; consequently there was no reason to explain away, by exegetical subtlety, the reference to the *Boanerges* or *Sons of Thunder* amongst the disciples of Our Lord. The real difficulty arose out of the observation of an apparent parallel between Jesus in the Gospels and Jason in the Argonautica. Could we assume the equivalence of Jesus and Jason etymologically? Was Jason originally a Semitic product, borrowed, as so many other Oriental features, by the Greeks? If so, was it possible that the Gospel, either in its central figure or its leading incidents, had been Jasonised? If not Jasonised, might we say Dioscurised? As regards Jason, it was made out that the Jason-Cult was widely diffused in Asia, but the final evidence for his Semitic ancestry is not yet forthcoming. It seems more probable that the home of the hero was in Thessaly or in Crete than in Palestine. So the identification to which we have referred is covered at present by a suspense of judgement. Dioscurism, however, is a much more widely diffused factor than Jasonism, and there is reason to suspect that its influence may be capable of detection in the New Testament, beyond the playful cognomen given to the Sons of Zebedee. It will require a good deal of patient investigation to define the limits within which the influence has operated.

We come now to the outlook of the present volume. The discovery of the Aryan Twins, the Sanskrit Açvins or Nasatiya, upon the Hittite Monuments, would lead naturally enough to the enquiry as to whether traces of Twin-cult exist among the populations who now occupy the ground of the ancient Hittite Empire. An accidental discovery made it possible to carry such an enquiry out to a definite conclusion, and to show that in the region in question, and down to a time at least as late as the second century of the Christian era, twins were regarded as the sons or the priests of the Thunder-god, and that such a twin-priest received the name Barlaha or Son of God; this startling discovery occupies the front place in the present volume[1].

After that we return to Zeus, who is now resolved into the Thunder-bird (the Woodpecker), the Thunder-tree, and the Thunder-bolt, or axe. The question of the diffusion of Woodpecker-cult is taken up afresh, and it is asked whether in the British Isles there are traces of Woodpecker-cult or of Twin-cult at special centres. The results are again surprising; for it can be shown that, all over England, there are traces of the deference paid to the Woodpecker.

In this way the argument proceeds, and the results of the previous volumes become more and more accentuated and assured. It is not easy to say how much further this reconstruction of primitive religion is likely to go: it is already long past the stage

---

[1] The chapter is reprinted from Preuschen's *Zeitschrift für N. T. Wissenschaft* for 1914, where it formed a part of a votive number to Julius Wellhausen on his seventieth birthday.

of the incredulous jest with which it was at first received, even by some who were folk-lorists of high repute; the proved human interest in twins and their destruction cannot be limited to the question "which of them shall I keep?" We are confident also that the supposition on the part of some unsympathetic readers (if indeed they were actual readers) that the writer with whom they professed to be acquainted saw everything double, will not much longer be found satisfactory to educated people. However let them say what they will. The present volume shows that we are continuing the investigation. It is a part of the Quest for Truth to which we have been all our lives committed.

R. H.

February 1916.

TABLE OF CONTENTS

CHAPTER I

ON THE NAME "SON OF GOD" IN NORTHERN SYRIA

An inscription in Greek characters was recently sent me by my friend Professor Lootfy Levonian, of the American College at 'Ain Ṭab, which ran as follows:

BAPΛAA
[Figure of an eagle]
AΛYΠЄ XAI
PЄ
ЄTOYCZΛY

i.e. Βαρλάα, ἄλυπε χαῖρε· ἔτους ζλυ'.

This inscription may serve as the point of departure for the following investigation; it does not contain anything which cannot be paralleled from other quarters, but it contains within its own brief compass several important statements, from which equally important inferences can be drawn; so we will begin by considering it from the side of epigraphic lore.

In the first place, then, it is a funeral inscription. This appears from the conjunction of the name of the person (a) with the figure of an eagle, a common funerary symbol in northern Syria[1], (b) with a common form of Greek farewell to the departed, (c) with a date which is presumably the date of death.

The next thing we notice is that although the inscription is in Greek, the name of the deceased is transliterated from the Syriac; he is called Bar ᵊaʾlāhā, or Son of God. It is, therefore, the grave of a Syrian. When we have recognised this indisputable fact, of which, strange as it may seem that a Syrian should have such a name, we shall find abundance of confirmation and parallel, we may perhaps be able to clear up an obscurity as to the date.

---

[1] Cumont has written at length on the subject of the " Funerary Eagle among the Syrians" in *Revue de l'Histoire des Religions* for 1910.

For if the deceased is of Syrian family (though the family were bilingual and had Greek for a second language), the stone-cutter of the inscription is probably a Syrian, and that would explain why he has written the figures of the date in reverse order, so as to give the year ζλυ′, where he should have written υλζ′, i.e. the year 437 of the Seleucid era, corresponding to the Christian date A.D. 125–6[1].

The inscription itself was found not very far from ‘Ain Ṭab, and we may, therefore, describe it as a funeral inscription from Commagene in the early part of the second century (the date depending upon the accuracy of the transcription and its interpretation, which I do not think admit of serious question). We shall see presently reasons for believing that it cannot be very far wrong, for we shall be able to refer other Bar-Alaha inscriptions to the same period, and to connect them, directly or indirectly, with the same locality. The Greek formula ἄλυπε χαῖρε need not detain us long; in this shape and in a somewhat more extended one ἄωρε καὶ ἄλυπε χαῖρε we find it in use in the East: I quote an instance from a Palmyrene bust in the possession of a sheikh at Kuryatein, on the road to Palmyra, which appears in Lidzbarski[2] in the following form:

Greek	Palmyrene
NACPAΛ	נצרא בר
ΛΑΘΕΜΑΛ	מלכו בר
ΧΟΥΑΛΥΠΕ	נצרא חבל
ΧΑΙΡΕ	

where the Greek is deciphered by Lidzbarski as follows:

Νασράλλαθε Μάλχου ἄλυπε χαῖρε:

the Palmyrene showing simply *Naṣra, son of Malku, son of Nasra*,

---

[1] Such lapidary reversals are common on the Palmyrene monuments. Cf. Lidzbarski, *Handbuch*: "Palmyrene Inscriptions," I. p. 458 *et sqq.* where are the Greek dates:

> ἔτους νυ′ = A.D. 139.
> ἔτους Ϙυ′ = A.D. 179.
> ἔτους δφ′ = A.D. 193.
> ἔτους δνφ′ = A.D. 242–3, etc.,

and which dates are certified by the Palmyrene texts. The same thing occurs in the trilingual inscription from Zebed, whose date is given, in words, in the Syriac as 823 (i.e. of the Seleucid era), but in Greek in the form ἔτους γκω′ (328).

[2] Lidzbarski, II. 450.

mourning. The two sides are independent, the Palmyrene giving only the names: but it is reasonable that the names on the two sides should agree. It is quite impossible that the person buried should be called Νασράλλαθος, but he may very well have borne the name Νασράλλα or *Aquila Dei*, in which case we have a suggestive parallel to our Barlaha inscription[1]. The Greek of this inscription, however, needs to be re-examined. We will only use it at present to show how the Greek funeral formulae assert themselves in a bilingual country.

Here is another instance from Membidj (Hierapolis) which lies much nearer to 'Ain Ṭab[2].

Βάκχιε χρηστὲ ἄλυπε χαῖρε· Βκ΄ Γορπιαίου· β...

In this inscription we have again the conjunction of the funerary eagle with the Greek formula; and whether we take βκ to represent the Seleucid year or the day of the month (it is almost certainly the latter) the lapidary has again written his figures in the Semitic order, and is therefore probably a Syrian. If the day of the month be the 22nd, then the year which follows and begins with β has also its figures reversed.

Now for a word with regard to the bird whom Cumont calls the funerary eagle. It is commonly represented as holding a crown or garland in its beak, as a symbol of triumph and of the attainment of an immortal life among the blessed. In this form, for example, it is a constant motive upon the tombs at Membidj, the ancient Hierapolis of which Lucian writes. Similar things may be remarked at Balkis on the Euphrates, which Cumont holds to be the real Zeugma (commonly identified with Biredjik), where the road from 'Ain Ṭab crossed the Euphrates: so that we may see that, in this part of Syria, the funerary eagle is conventional; Cumont maintains further that it was from the East that the Romans borrowed their idea of apotheosis of the Emperors, and the fiction that Romulus was carried up to heaven on the back of an eagle. It is probable that the problem of apotheosis by the help of eagles can be solved more simply: for if the eagle should turn out to be not a piece of Syrian ornithology, but the Thunder-bird itself, which turns up at the origin of all religions, he will not need to be imported into Rome from the East; he

---

[1] Perhaps Νασράλλαθε means that the stone-cutter began to write θεοῦ after Νασράλλα.

[2] It will be found in Cumont, *loc. cit.* p. 120, from Hogarth, *Annual of the British School at Athens* for 1907–8, pp. 186 *sqq.*

will be at home there already, just as he is in any place where his royalty has displaced the minor claims of the Woodpecker to be the bird-form of the Thunder.

We shall point out presently that in the case of our Barlaha inscription, the eagle has a nexus with Barlaha, quite independently of the fact that Barlaha happens to have died: of this we have more to say at a later point. The inscription is non-Christian; we should suspect this from the occurrence of a pagan and hopeless formula, and from the presence of the eagle; but we are quite certain that no Christian in the year 125 would ever have been designated by the title of Son of God, nor is it likely that the term could have been employed by the Jews. The problem before us, then, is to determine the meaning of this pagan formula of nomenclature. Who is the god that is indicated, and how does anyone come to be his son? What honours attach to such sonship and what functions does the son discharge? And by what marks, if any, is he recognised? Is it royalty that is meant by the term, or is it priesthood? Or does the title depend upon physical and moral characteristics? These, and similar questions, are the points that require to be considered; and it will easily be seen that there are similar questions in most of the great religions, and in not a few of the small ones. The relation of kingship, for example, interpreted as sonship, is common in the earlier Judaism: the Psalms are full of it; "Thou art my Son, this day have I begotten thee[1]," is an adoptionist formula in the older religion, which became an adoptionist formula in the Christian religion: and again, as the writer to the Hebrews would say, "I will be to him a father and he shall be to me a son[2]." The same exact terms of adoptionism are found in Ps. lxxxix. 27, "I will make him my first-born, the highest of the kings of the earth." In all these cases the king is regarded as, by adoption, the Son of God. What is true of Judaism is true of the Syrian Kingdom of Damascus, where we find a decided tendency to name their kings Bar-hadad, that is, to define them as the children of the Thunder-god; for Hadad (Adad) is the Amorite and Mesopotamian god of the Thunder: and in that sense, a Syrian king so named might be called in the terms of a later day, Son of God.

It is, however, useless to look in this direction for the meaning of Barlaha, for in the first place the country is under Roman rule,

[1] Ps. ii. 7.   [2] 2 Sam. vii. 14. Heb. i. 5.

and there are no more kings to be affiliated to the gods, and in the next place, as we shall see, the name in question is borne by persons who are politically civilians. Our humble inscription is certainly not the tombstone of a king. Perhaps we shall reach a solution most easily by removing our attention for a while from the first syllable of the name, and fixing it on the remainder. Whatever sonship may mean, there is no question as to the meaning of the word Alaha. What god is meant by this title in Commagene in the year 125 A.D.? The answer to this enquiry is certain: if any god is especially indicated by the name Son of God, it should be the one whom archaeologists know as Jupiter Dolichenus, i.e. the Jupiter worshipped at Dolichē, a town a few hours to the north of 'Ain Ṭab, represented to-day by a wretched Moslem village known as Tell Dülük, with many ruined walls and an occasional Syrian inscription, indicating obscurely the former greatness of the town. This town, whose ruins I have visited, though with no prospect of making excavations, has impressed itself on the whole western world, chiefly by means of its religion, which soldiers from Commagene carried as far as England, Scotland and Wales, Gaul, Germany, Pannonia, Dacia, and Numidia, to say nothing of countries lying nearer to the centre of civilisation. In fact, Commagene became a recruiting ground of the Antonine emperors, and the soldiers who were thus incorporated with the Roman army carried their religious symbols with them wherever they went, adapting themselves skilfully to the nomenclature of the Roman religion, so as to call their chief deity by the name of Jupiter, and establishing shrines and votive monuments wherever they travelled, much in the same way as did the worshippers of Mithras. The extent of the Dolichene influence can be judged by the number of inscriptions belonging to the cult. Hardly one has been found as yet in Commagene itself (though no doubt they will turn up when Tell Dülük is excavated), but apart from Commagene they are found all over the Roman Empire. Who then is Jupiter Dolichenus, for it is certain that in an ancient Eastern province, which has formed part of some of the greatest empires of the world, he was not called Jupiter, nor was he known by a place-name such as Dolichenus? The answer is that he is a survival from Hittite and Assyrian days. In some ways he resembles the Hittite storm-god Teshub; in others he is like the Amorite Adad, or Hadad, the thunder-god of Northern Mesopotamia, or the

Assyrian Ramman, the storm-god of the great empires on the two rivers. From the fact that he is always represented with the double-axe (thunder-axe), in his right hand, and with the bunch of split lightnings in his left, we might be disposed to say that he was simply the Thunder-god of the population of this region, slightly Romanised into a Jupiter Optimus Maximus, and accompanied by such religious symbols as we are accustomed to in the Thunder-cults of the East and West. Closer examination shows, however, that the matter is not so simple; for although the figure of Jupiter Dolichenus himself, in the monuments of the cult, is undoubtedly that of a thunder-god, there are features which suggest that he is Sky-god as well as Thunder-god, exactly as was the case with Zeus himself, who obtains his name from the bright sky, and discharges the functions of the darkened sky. In the Dolichene cult, we shall find the central figure accompanied by lesser figures of the Sun and Moon, sometimes associated with a pair of stars. Sometimes a feminine goddess is added, who passes for Juno, and may be the wife of the Solar deity. The denomination of the cult as that of a thunder-god is, therefore, not exhaustive. The main idea is certainly that of the Thunder. Jupiter Dolichenus stands on the back of a bull marching from left to right, the bull being his cult-symbol, as it is for Ramman in Assyria; he has the thunder-eagle with him, sometimes perched on the head of the bull, sometimes crouching beneath it, as if to support it, and sometimes flying with garlands symbolic of victory; and as we have said, he always carries the thunder-axe and the bunch of lightnings.

The god, therefore, who is involved in the name Barlaha must be sought for amongst the thunder-gods and sky-gods of the Oriental peoples. That being the case, the nearest equivalent that we can find in ancient history for the term Barlaha is the name Bar-Hadad (the Benhadad of the Hebrew Bible). Kingship being, however, excluded as an explanation, we must now try priesthood. It is well known that priests commonly acquire theophoric names, expressive of their relation to the God whom they serve; sometimes they actually pose under the name of the god himself. Let us, then, see whether we can make a priest of Barlaha.

In an inscription, preserved in the Museum at Salona in Dalmatia, we find the following[1]:

[1] C.I.L. iii. Suppl. ii. 8785.

D(is) M(anibus) | Aurelius Ger|manus Barla|ha
Sacerdos | I(ovis) O(ptimi) M(aximi) Doli|cheni
vivus | sibi posuit et | Syre coniugi |

Figure of a double-axe.

Here there is a votive inscription for the tomb of a priest of
Jupiter Dolichenus named Barlaha, with his wife, whose name is
simply Syra or Syre, the Syrian lady; and the inscription is
accompanied by the symbol of the thunder. It is clear, then,
that a priest of Jupiter Dolichenus might be named Barlaha; it
does not follow that every one named Barlaha is necessarily a
priest of Dolichenus; and it seems to be made out that the Alaha
of the Commagene Barlaha really does mean someone attached
to Jupiter Dolichenus, or the thunder-god (sky-god) who lies
behind him.

Let us now try to find out some more about this Dolichene
priesthood; for if the priests are in the habit of wearing theophoric
names, as in the instance before us, we may find from the inscriptions some more information about the cult than is betrayed by
a scrutiny and study of the surviving Dolichene sculptures.
The simplest way to determine what were the favourite names of
Dolichene priests is to work through the collection of the inscriptions of the cult in Kan, *De Jovis Dolicheni cultu.* We shall
easily detect five varieties of appellation (omitting names which
are clearly Roman, and generally imperial, like Flavius or Antoninus
and the like). These five varieties are as follows:

1.   Those priests who bear the name Marinus or Marianus:
2.   those who bear the names Castor and Polydeuces:
3.   the priestly name of Barlaha:
4.   the name Barsamya:
5.   the name Aquila.

All of these names are those of priests attached to the service of
the god, and they have, to say the least, a theophoric flavour.
The evidence is as follows, the numbers of the inscriptions being
as in Kan.

No. 3.   *Polydeuces* Theophili along with Lucius Capito and Flavius
Reginus.
No. 4.   *Castor* and *Aquila* with *Castor* and *Polydeuces*.
No. 11.   Aelius Valentinus veteranus sacerdos.
No. 14.   *Marinus Mariani* Bassus.
No. 15.   Aurelius *Marinus* with *Adde bar Semei* and *Oceanus* Socratis.
No. 17.   Bassus *Aquila* and Gai Gaiani.

No. 22.   Aurelius Germanus *Barlaha ut supra*.
No. 26.   Aurelii Sabinianus et Maximus et Apollinarius.
No. 33.   Aurelius Domittius with the brethren
Flavius *Castor* and⎫
Aurelius Maximus⎭ brothers, not said positively to be priests.
No. 44.   Antonius.
No. 48.   Antiochus and *Marinus*.
No. 53.   Bellicus *Marini* filius sacerdos.
No. 59.   Demittius sacerdos.
No. 64.   Sacerdotibus.   Sopatrus et *Marinus* et Calus (sic).
No. 67.   C. Julius *Marinus* miles, not said to be a priest.
No. 70.   Flavius *Marinus* and Chrysas Thyrsus.
No. 72.   C. Fabius Germanus.
No. 75.   Aurelius Severus veteranus curator tempuli (in Aventino) et
Aurelius Antiochus sacerdos, etc.
No. 83.   M. Ulfius Chresimus.
No. 84.   Aurelius *Teatecnus filius Hela*.
No. 86.   Aurelius Julianus eques Romanus sacerdos.
No. 99.   Antipatrus sacerdos.
No. 100. Marcus *Barsemias*.
Nos. 104 and 105.   C. Julius Flaccus.
No. 106. L. Aurelius Valerius.
No. 136. Arcias *Marinus*.
No. 141. G. Julius *Marinus* (not said to be a priest).
No. 152. Lucinus (?) Donatii, *Aquila Barsemon* and Flavius Damas.

It will be seen at a glance that these lists of priestly names are significant. Setting aside a number of imperatorial names of the time, we have, for the most part, a series of theophoric names, which belong to the Dolichene religion, and will help us to understand the nature of the cult. Of these the first is Marinus and its associated Marianus. The name stands for an old Syriac form *Marin*, and its companion *Maryan*: each formed from the word Mari, which becomes Mar in later Syriac (with silent *yud*), by the addition of a suffix in the first person plural. The meaning is then "our Lord," and it is an archaic title of honour, probably used both for priests and kings. It becomes the appellation of saints in the Eastern Church. It does not appear from our list of cases that it is exclusively a priestly title, nor that it must be necessarily read in a theophoric sense, though one remembers how common is the doctrine that the honour of the priest is as the honour of God. As it happens, in one case Marinus is described as a soldier, and therefore presumably not a priest[1]. Other

[1] This statement may require qualification; we do not know whether Dolichene priests accompanied the Syrian legions into foreign countries. Some

instances of similar character can be brought forward. Students of Philo will remember the way in which the mob in Alexandria made a mock king of the poor idiot Carabas and saluted him with cries of Marin. Here the name has its loftiest connotation. We can, however, find a number of persons of humble origin, who bear the name without any sense of elevation or dignity. It appears to have become conventional[1].

The next case is more striking: we have Castor and Pollux in conjunction, and Castor several times separately. There can be no mistake about the meaning of this; the Heavenly Twins are a part of the Dolichene priesthood: and we must conclude that the cult involved not merely the Sky or the Thunder, but the Children of the Sky and the Children of the Thunder. Such priests are in all probability twins, or are acting representatively in a line of priests who have the care of a twin-cult. (A good instance is the priest Amphion at Antioch, for whom Tiberius set up the monument of Zethus and Amphion.) Now this might have been divined: for in Commagene we are in the Hittite country; and it is known from the inscriptions found at Boghaz köi, that the Hittites had not only a thunder-god (Teshub)˙ but that there was also in the vicinity of the Hittite empire, and perhaps within the empire itself, a pair of twin deities who are called by their Aryan name Nasatiyau in the treaties between the Hittites, the Mitanni, etc. Thus every reason for regarding the cult of Jupiter Dolichenus as a survival, is a reason for expecting the survival of the cult of the Twins.

In the light of this important discovery of the existence of a twin element in the Dolichene priesthood, we may ask whether this fact can be used to illustrate the monuments. The answer priestly functions may have been discharged by soldiers; e.g. in the inscription from the Aventine (No. 75 in Kan) the curator of the temple is expressly said to be a *veteranus*. So in the inscription No. 11 of Kan, Aelius Valentinus is expressly said to be both *veteranus* and *sacerdos*. In No. 53 Bellicus the priest is almost certainly a soldier; from the description of him as *Filius Marini* it is possible that his father may have been a priest also. In No. 67 we have another soldier named Marinus, who may suggest a similar explanation.

Hettner, *De Jove Dolicheno*, p. 9, says that the cognomen Marinus is found much more often in Dolichene inscriptions than can be explained by chance; as in not less than seven instances the name is that of a priest, he concludes that the Dolichene Marini are connected with the cult.

[1] E.g. at the end of the Edessan Acts of Sharbil, we are told that Marinus was one of the notaries who composed the document. But perhaps this is consistent with dignity.

is that the pair of stars in the Dolichene monuments must be held to be symbols of the Twins. Are the Twins themselves represented? Not in the Roman or Greek form; it is possible that the sun or the moon may have come in to represent the Twins as they do in some Assyrian inscriptions. What seems to confirm the supposed Assyrian influence at this point is the fact that the Dolichene monuments sometimes represent the Sun and Moon as carrying whips. Now the whip is from India westward a well-known Dioscuric symbol. The following sentence from Mr A. B. Cook's recently published *Zeus* will illustrate the point[1]. He is describing one of the Dolichene plates found at Heddernheim :

The upper division contains a bust of Sarapis; the lower, busts of the Sun and Moon. The Sun has the horns of a bull; the Moon, a rayed nimbus: *both bear whips. Over their heads are two stars.*

Without laying too much stress on this point, we can see that the reference to Castor and Polydeuces amongst the Dolichene priesthood requires us to admit that the Twins are a fundamental part of the cult, and that their presence on the monument is not due to syncretism[2].

But what were their names in Syriac, for after all, Castor and Pollux can only be a translation? It is possible that they may have had names which have come down to us as Cosmas and Damian, the ecclesiastical substitute for the Twins in this region, but we have not the means of determining this at present. The names Cosmas (Cosmus) and Damas are both found on the Dolichene monuments, and Damas appears to be a priest. That is as far as we can go with what, for the present, is little more than a suggestion.

There is, however, remarkable evidence in our list of the currency of the word Twin as a name. Twin, in Syriac, as is well known, is *Tauma*, and the similarity of this to the word for Abyss or Ocean (*Tehoma*), led earlier compilers of Onomastica to derive the name Thomas (or twin) from *Abyssus*. In the same way when pious persons attempted to get rid of the statement in the

[1] *Loc. cit.* I p. 620.

[2] Thus, when we find upon a Roman inscription (No. 71, Kan) that it is dedicated to J(ovi) O(ptimo) s(ancto) p(raestantissimo) D(olicheno) et Junoni Sanctae Herae Castoribus et Apollini, we are to regard all these as Roman equivalents for figures in the Dolichene cult. Juno as Hera is a double substitution; Apollo is the Sun-god of the east, and the Castors are the Twins.

On the inscription No. 91 of Kan, Juno is expressly called *Juno Assyria regina Dolichena.*

Syriac Acts of Thomas that Judas Thomas was the Twin of the Messiah, they did it by substituting the Abyss, or (as Wright translates it) the Ocean-flood of the Messiah. Now notice that in our list of priestly names, one man has actually given his name as *Oceanus* Socratis. It is safe to say that no one ever had such a name in the course of nature: it has come to him artificially; it is translator's Latin, and bad translation at that. In his own country, this priest would have been called Twin, or perhaps Thomas[1].

Our next case is the name with which we started, Bar Alaha, which we have sufficiently explained. Look, however, at No. 84, where Teatecnus (*read* Theotecnos = θεότεκνος) occurs. Evidently Theotecnos is an attempt to turn Bar Alaha into Greek: nor is this all; another translation is given into Latin, for the inscription says Teatecnus *filius Hela*, which is only a blundering Latin version of Barlaha by someone who forgot that Alaha was written backward. We shall find this name Theotecnos (Theotecna) in the Edessan literature. In the story of the Martyrdom of Habib the Deacon in the year A.D. 308, mention is made of a certain Theotecna, a veteran and a chief of the governor's band. Although a pagan, he shows himself friendly to Habib. There is nothing definitely to intimate priesthood: he appears to have been simply a military official. On the other hand, we have already pointed out a case in Rome, where the *veteranus* Aurelius Severus is said to have been the warden of the Dolichene temple on the Aventine, and another Italian case of a *veteranus* who is definitely described as *sacerdos*.

So here again we have the Dolichene priest as Son of God, with a possible parallel from the not far distant city of Edessa. The priest in question has sought to render this both in Latin and Greek. Such translations are not mere western adaptations, they occur in Commagene, which is a bilingual country, and to some extent trilingual.

The next sacerdotal name occurs under slightly variant forms:

Adde bar Semei,

Marcus Barsemias,

and   Aquila Barsemon,

the three forms are evidently for one Syriac name, which must be "bar Šemaya (Son of the Sky)." Here then the Dolichene Alaha

---

[1] Hettner, p. 10, thinks that both Marinus and Oceanus may be variant translations of a Syriac word (=lat. *mare*). We have explained Marin above, and shown that it is altogether Syriac.

is definitely recognised as the Sky-god. The alternative explanation Bar Samaya, son of the blind man, is untenable: we could
not have three sons of blind men in our list: but the alternative
should be noted because it explains the name of the Edessan
bishop Barsamya, who is said to have been the second catholic
bishop of Edessa and successor of Palut. We must take this
Barsamya to be a Christianisation of an original Bar Šemaya.
The Edessan traditions refer him to the times of Fabian, Pope of
Rome, and so before 250 A.D. He is probably a convert from
paganism.

The name Adde is also Syriac; it is = Addai, the supposed
apostle of the church at Edessa. It is itself perhaps a thunder-name.

Last of all we have three cases of Aquila as a proper name.
In view of the connection of the names already discussed with the
cult, it is reasonable to suggest that the priest, who bears the
name, bears it theophorically, because of the companionship of
the eagle with the thunder.

We have now discussed the character of the Dolichene priesthood, the god being accompanied by twins as his assessors, and
perhaps by a feminine conjugate. At Commagene, at all events,
if any one comes forward with the name Son of God, we identify
him as either a priest of the Thunder, or a twin-child of the
Thunder, or both.

Reviewing the argument as far as it has gone, we have arrived
at the following facts:

A bilingual inscription from Commagene commemorates a
Syrian bearing the name Son-of-God, who died in the year 125 A.D.
The god after whom he is named must be identified with Jupiter
Dolichenus. We actually find the name as a priest's name in the
cult in question. On studying the names of Dolichene priests
which have come down to us in inscriptions, we find that they
were called by such names as the following, all of which express
their relation to the cult: *Our Lord, Son of God, Heavenly Twin,
Son of the Sky, Twin, Eagle (of God ?)*. The Dolichene cult was,
therefore, a twin-cult as well as a sky-cult and a thunder-cult,
and the Twins, who here turn up with Zeus, have come down out
of ancient times as the Children of the Sky or the assessors of the
Thunder. This discovery is important for the study of Twin-cult
in Western Asia; it might have been anticipated from the discovery
of the Aryan twins on Hittite monuments.

We have now to cross the Euphrates, in order to find out whether the Barlaha phenomenon reappears in Mesopotamia, and, in particular, in the district Osroene with its capital Edessa. We must be prepared for a change of values in religious symbols when we enter Edessa; for here the Sky counts for more and the Thunder for less. Edessan worship is largely solar, and the twins who are the solar assessors (Monim and Aziz) are almost certainly the Morning and Evening Stars. Alongside of this there appear traces of old Assyrian worship, but not especially of Ramman or Adad so much as of Bel and Nebo. The first impression is that, on entering Mesopotamia, we have left the Thunder behind us. This is not really the case, for down to the sixth century we can find traces of Thunder-cult. One very interesting example will be found in the Scholia of Theodore Bar Koni[1]. He describes a sect in the district of Gozan who worship thunder, and are called Barqayē (i.e. People of the Lightning):

Barqa is not that which dazzles in the clouds, but once upon a time there was a man at Rkem in Gaya, who was called Barqin. He was rich but childless and he made for himself a statue which he called the Thunder (Lightning) of the people of Gozan.

Upon which Pognon notes that from what Theodore Bar Koni says, we must conclude that down to his day, or not long before his day, the people of the district of Gozan worshipped a deity whom they called Barqa (the Lightning).

Evidently Bar Koni was puzzled by the accounts given to him of certain Lightning-worshippers: he suggests explanations as to the importation of the statue of the Thunder from abroad, and that it was not really the Thunder, but a certain Mr Thunder. We need not doubt the existence of a Mesopotamian sect of Thunder-worshippers in the sixth century of our era.

Now let us come to Edessa, and see what we find that is analogous to the Barlaha priest in the district of Commagene. We have already stumbled upon one parallel, viz. the case of the veteran Theotecnos, who turns up in the story of the Martyrdom of Habib the deacon. Theotecnos is, as we have shown, a Dolichene translation of Barlaha, and there is good probability that the name had the same significance in Edessa. We can, moreover, actually find traces of the name Barlaha untranslated in Edessa.

---

[1] I quote the Scholia from Pognon, *Coupes de Khouabir*, Part II. Append. II.

First of all, there was a gate of the city called the gate of
Barlaha; and second, there was a sanctuary outside the city called
by the name of Beth Mar[1] Barlaha.

Professor Wright, in his edition of the Chronicle of Joshua the
Stylite, reproduces Carsten Niebuhr's map of Edessa[1] with corrections from Prof. Hoffmann: in this map we find the gate of
Barlaha placed, with some hesitation, on the north of the city.
As to the sanctuary of Barlaha, which should be connected, one
would think, with the gate of the same name, we are in some
difficulty, for it is clearly a Christian sanctuary, and Barlaha has
the prefixed Mar[1] of the Christian dignity, and ought therefore to
be a Christian saint, unless we take this Mar[1] also to be a survival
from a pagan Marin, such as was suggested by the Dolichene
inscriptions.   Thus we have the perplexity of finding a Christian
Barlaha, which appears to contradict what we said of the occurrence of the name in Commagene as a definitely pagan religious
name.   Let us see what authorities we have for the Son-of-God
Sanctuary.

We find in the Edessan Chronicle the following statement:
"In the year 720 (= A.D. 409) Mar Diogenes became Bishop of
Edessa.   He began to build the sanctuary of Barlaha."   Upon
which Hallier notes[2] that nothing is known as to the situation of
this shrine.   The odd thing about this bishop and his building
is that his own name is a Greek equivalent of Barlaha!   Later
references in the Edessene Chronicle only tell us of more bishops
being buried there, as if it were a kind of episcopal mausoleum.

In the year 525 A.D. Bishop Asklepios of Edessa died in Antioch
and was buried there; his body was translated in the same year
to Edessa, and buried in Beth Mar[1] Barlaha, along with Bishop
Nonnus.   In the year 532 A.D., on Dec. 6th, died Bishop Andreas,
and was buried with Bishop Nonnus and Bishop Asklepios in
Beth Mar[1] Barlaha.

The sanctuary must have been a place of some importance,
at least from the beginning of the fifth century.   There appears
to be no knowledge of any saint or martyr after whom it could
have been named.   The natural suggestion is that it was a pagan
sanctuary converted to Christian uses, and that Barlaha was

----

[1] *Voyage en Arabie et en d'autres Pays circumvoisins*, traduit de l'Allemand,
1780 II. p. 330.

[2] *Edessenische Chronik*, p. 106.

either a pagan priest or one of the Heavenly Twins. He may even have been the Bishop Diogenes himself, in a pre-Christian state of existence.

Certainly something like this transfer and modification of pagan terms and cults appears to have taken place in the case of Barsamya, one of the earliest of the Edessan martyrs. Here the Commagene parallel is very close, where we found three separate modifications of the name Bar Šemaya, the Son of the Sky. We have no means of testing the historical value of the Barsamya legends, but if we have conjectured rightly the meaning of the name, it is not very far from Son of the Sky to Son of God. Both names would, in this view, belong to a pagan cult of the Sky and the Heavenly Bodies.

There is another reason for believing that in Edessa Barlaha is a pagan name with a pagan meaning. We can actually find a sepulchral inscription containing the feminine form of the name Barlaha. Readers of my *Cult of the Heavenly Twins* will find a photograph of a sepulchral mosaic, recently discovered on the north of the City of Edessa. It has now been transferred to the museum of Constantinople. It contains a series of portraits of Aphthoniya (if Prof. Burkitt's correction of my first reading be taken) and of his family. This Aphthoniya (or Aphthonius) is the person who is commemorated on one of the Twin Pillars of Edessa as having set up the pillar for Shalmath the Princess. We are discussing what may be described as the central mosaic in a royal mausoleum. The portraits in the mosaic are grouped as follows, with names attached:

Shumu.	Aphthoniya bar Garmu.
Asu.	Garmu.
Shalmath (Inscription).	Barthlaha.

Clearly this must be regarded as a pagan sepulchre: for two of the persons mentioned in it are connected with the setting up of the Twin Pillars, which cannot be a Christian function. The inscription, too, in which Aphthoniya records the making of the sepulchre for himself and his family, has nothing Christian about it. We may, therefore, feel sure that Barthlaha is a pagan name, and is the exact conjugate of Barlaha which we have been discussing. We cannot speak positively as to how she became entitled to the name Daughter-of-God, i.e. Daughter of the Sky. It does not seem likely *à priori* that she was a priestess, though this is not impossible; perhaps the simplest explanation is that she obtained this name because she was a twin.   It seems probable that when this sepulchre was made, Edessa was still pagan.

Reviewing the course of the enquiry, the evidence seems to point to a pagan Sky-cult in Edessa: we have drawn attention to (a) Theotecnos; (b) to Barsamya, probably a Christian modification of an original Son of the Sky; (c) to the occurrence of Barlaha as the name of a gate and of a sanctuary at Edessa; (d) to the actual occurrence of the feminine Barthlaha in a pagan sepulchre.

Our real difficulty was to see how such a name as Barlaha could have passed into Christian use at all.   It would almost be blasphemous to a Christian of the Nicene days, if used as a personal appellation.   The case of Barhadad is not quite an exact parallel. We are able to find a Christian Bishop of Tella in the sixth century bearing the name Barhadad.   His story is told in the Chronicle of Joshua the Stylite.   This name might, however, have become colourless, through the disuse of any reference to Hadad as a deity: it was not much worse than Diogenes.   But Barlaha could never lose its meaning, as long as Syriac continued to be spoken, and the meaning must have been offensive to Christian ears.

The total impression produced on the mind by the enquiry is that Barlaha, as a personal name, in Edessa, has the same meaning as it had in Commagene, with the exception that the deity involved is the Sky-god rather than the Thunder-god.   The next thing to be done is to examine whether traces of similar cults and nomenclatures of priesthoods or twins can be found in other districts, and especially in Palestine or the adjacent countries.

CHAPTER II

We now return to the Woodpecker-cult with the object of finding out whether there are any traces of Twin-cult centres or Woodpecker sanctuaries in the British Isles.

Our investigation into the place of the Woodpecker in Greek and Roman religion has taught us how to proceed. We ascertained, for example, that there was a town in Attica, called Keleai, ruled over by a certain King Keleos, who had twin children, named Jason (or Jasion) and Triptolemos, and who was on terms of friendship and hospitality with Demeter. Since Keleos is the Green Woodpecker, and twins are involved in the legend, we identify Keleai as a twin-town. It is a not unnatural supposition, judging from West African parallels, to suggest that Keleai might have been Twin-village to Eleusis, or even to Athens. However that may be, the identification tells us to look for the cult-centres in places named after the Thunder-bird or the Thunder, or in places that have a traditional connection with Twins. The same kind of enquiry would be made, if the town in question had been named after the twins, instead of their sire.

In Italy we do not always have the evidence before us in complete form. Picenum is certainly a Woodpecker town, and the legends of Picenum tell us that the Woodpecker was actually worshipped on a pillar as the guide of the original emigrants who founded the city. As we have no Picene history we cannot be certain that Twins were involved in the foundation, but there is a probability that the Picus of Picenum is parallel to the Keleos of Keleai, and that the emigration under the leadership of the

Woodpecker was in reality an exile of persons under the Twin and Woodpecker taboo[1]. In the case of Rome the evidence is more nearly complete: the twins are there, and the woodpecker parents on the sacred tree: the sanctuary also is, as Livy shows us, part of the primitive Roman tradition. We do not yet know the meaning of Rome, or of Romulus (Romus) and Remus, but that does not prevent us from a convincing identification of Rome as a Twin-town and a Woodpecker-town.

Now let us turn to Northern Europe, and in particular to the British Isles.

Following the analogy of Eleusis (i.e. Keleai) and Picenum, we should naturally look for places that are named after the Woodpecker, including places that are named after the Thunder, in later than bird-form. If such places exist, they may be sufficiently numerous to convince us that we are dealing with a cult, and with centres at which the cult is practised. In the same way we may, apart from places, find persons who bear a name that is directly or indirectly borrowed from the Woodpecker or the Thunder: if such names were to occur frequently we should suspect that they had a religious meaning: and especially if the personal names turned out to be place-names as well, we should put down the inferred place-names as cult-centres or sanctuaries. This, then, is the direction in which we have to look, and it is not one that at first sight seems promising of good results. For in the first place, the etymology either of localities or of persons has been a hunting-ground for the unscientific, whose zeal for foregone conclusion was equal to their ignorance of philology: and in the next place, those persons who have been studying philologically the place-names of the British Isles (and the same thing is true of the personal names) have almost nothing to offer us as the results of what has been in many cases a painstaking and scientific investigation.

During the past few years a number of excellent monographs have appeared dealing with the place-names of various counties

---

[1] We may, however, show that the case of Picenum was not peculiar. The same feature occurs among the people of Latium whom the Romans called *Aborigines*, where we have the oracle of the bird described alternatively as an oracle of Mars. On the one hand this leads us to infer that in Rome "Picus was also Mars," and therefore again we see that the Woodpecker is the parent of the Roman twins: on the other hand, the conjunction of Picus and Mars is suggested for Picenum, and this again suggests the twin-cult. See Dion. Hal. *Antiq.* I. 14.

and districts in England. My friend, the late Professor Skeat, was responsible for Cambridgeshire, Huntingdonshire, Bedford-shire, Hertfordshire and Berkshire[1]: but neither in these mono-graphs, nor in any of the studies of place-names of other counties which have been published (with one or two slight exceptions), does there appear to be any consciousness of the Woodpecker's existence, or any sense that he might, conceivably, have a right to exist. The only exceptions which I have noted thus far (without any pretence at completeness of acquaintance with possible forms) are as follows.

Goodall in his *Place-names of S.W. Yorkshire*, p. 138, remarks on the forms Fenay and Fenwick, that "the first element may be either OE *fin*, a plant-name, or OE *fina*, a woodpecker."

Again, on p. 167, he notes as follows:

Hickleton, Doncaster, DB Chicheltone, Icheltone, PF 1201 Hykelton, PC 1240 Hikilton, KI 1285 Hikylton. BCS has the place-name Hiceleswyrth which may be explained as "the farm of Hicel"[2]. It will be noted, however, that the early forms of Hickleton have neither -*s* nor -*e* to represent the genitive. Probably the name must therefore be explained as "woodpecker farm" from OE *Hicol*; see Middendorff.

The reference at the end is to Middendorff's *Altenglisches Flurnamenbuch*, p. 70, where we find as follows: "*hicol* st. m. Specht: ne.dial. hickol. æthiceles wyrðe 27 (vor a. 672)," i.e. *hicol* is a strong English masculine form and means wood-pecker: in neo-English dialect it is *hickol*: in the *Saxon Cartu-laries* of Birch, we find the place-name "æt hiceles wyrðe" (or

---

[1] To this I must now add the recent monograph on the place-names of Suffolk (A.D. 1913), which appears to have been his last published work. It is, in fact, posthumous. And here the Woodpecker is discovered, as the following extract will show (p. 46): "*Spexhall*. Copinger gives as old spellings such forms as *Speccyshale*, *Spectyshale* (obvious error for *Speccyshale*), *Spetteshale* (error for *Specceshale*), *Speckshall*. The suffix is clearly *hale*. The prefix can only take the form of Specces, gen. of an A.S.* Specc, which is unknown. If it were a name we should then have 'Speck's nook' as the sense. The E.D.D. says that *Speck* is the Norf. word for a woodpecker, which would represent an A.S.* *specc* and would be cognate with the German *Spech-t*. Kluge says that the E. *Speight*, a woodpecker, is borrowed from German, but thinks that the G. *Specht* may be allied to the A.S. *specca*, a speck; with reference to the parti-coloured plumage of the bird. My guess is that the name means 'woodpecker's nook'."

[2] The algebra of this is meant for experts: DB is the Domesday Book, PF stands for *Pedes finium*, PC for the *Pontefract Chartulary*, KI for *Kirkby's inquest*, BCS for Birch's *Cartularium Saxonicum*: the numbers represent the dates of the documentary evidence.

Hicklesworth) before the year A.D. 672[1]. I do not think there is any other writer on place-names who has made the same or a similar suggestion. Commonly the reference is made to a personal name *Finn,* to which a place-ending has been attached, or, for the other form quoted, and related forms, to a personal name *Hicel.* For example, Mutschmann, in his *Place-names of Nottinghamshire,* derives *Hickling* as "an O.E. patronymic: *æt* (*H*)*iclingum,* 'at the dwelling-place of the family of *Hicel.*' The *Iclingas* were a noble family to whom St Guthlac belonged. It is, however, by no means certain that *Hickling* was a settlement of that particular clan. The descendants of any man called *Hicel* would be called *Hicelingas.*"

There are, as we see in this typical example, no attempts to explain the hypothetical *Hicel.* It is clear that the Woodpecker, if he lies hidden under the forms alluded to, has not been recognised as a factor in English place-names, to any appreciable extent.

The same thing is also true of the personal names which are so closely involved in the names of places. It is unfortunate that the study of personal names is so far behind the study of place-names: it is still hardly out of the pre-scientific stage, where forms are explained by the imagination without regard to their history and development. Such a work as Bardsley's on *English Surnames* is an illustration of what we refer to. It is a mixture of pseudo-science and pious reflections. To do Bardsley justice, however, he must be credited with having discovered the Woodpecker as a personal name. For example, p. 495: "In our 'Woodalls,' 'Woodales' and 'Woodwalls,' not to say some of our 'Woodwells,' we are but reminded of the *woodwale,* the early woodpecker." After which the absurd addition is made that "Our 'Rains' are but the old 'Robert or William le Rain', another term for the same," because the Woodpecker is a rain-bird and prognosticates rain by its crying. No doubt the last statement is correct enough, but it will task the ingenuity of the imaginative to find a Woodpecker who is called, even popularly, le Rain[2].

---

[1] From Middendorff, apparently, came Goodall's other reference, if we may judge from the following (p. 51): "*fin,* Pflanzenname; Hauhechel, Ochsenkraut (ononis arvensis) ne. dial. fin; tô finlêage 627 (a. 909); finbeorh 992 (a. 957). *fina*; sw. m. Specht; fina; marsopicus, Ep. Gl. 648; tô finan mædwum 246 (um 780)."

[2] Mr Bardsley in his list of bird-names has also noted Speight, of which more anon.

Mr Moorman, in his valuable monograph on *W. Riding Place-Names*, introduces the Woodpecker-hypothesis only to reject it, e.g. p. vii:

To the student of local nomenclature it would seem at first sight as if these names (compounded with Eccle or Eccles) signified the hill, brook, ford, or enclosure of a man named Ecel, Eccel, or Æcel; and bearing in mind the modern dialect word *eckle*, meaning a green woodpecker, he might assume that O.E. Ecel, Eccel, or Æcel was a nickname, bestowed upon some early English settlers in the same way that other bird and beast and fish names were bestowed. But this interpretation of the place-names compounded with Eccles is open to two objections.

So Mr Moorman throws the Woodpecker over.

Since, then, we cannot find much done for us in the suggested enquiry by previous topographers, we must begin the investigation anew, with a full sense of the danger that besets us, of falling into the same philological traps that have been in the way of those who have preceded us.

A few stray notes have already appeared in the pages of *Boanerges*: it will be convenient to ignore these and begin the enquiry afresh.

In such an investigation our first care is to avoid dulness in the treatment of the theme. It would be easy to begin by gathering long lists of names of places that might reflect coincidences with possible names of the Woodpecker: but we would rather, in such an interesting enquiry, begin in a different way and leave the statistics and anything approaching to tabular record to the last stage of the study. The following appears to be the most attractive way of opening up the question.

Some time ago, when walking down the High Street of Guildford, my eyes fell upon a name which stood over one of the leading houses of business; the name which caught my attention was an unusual one, which I had never noticed before; it is a common amusement with me to try and unravel the names which are on the sign-boards of the streets through which one passes. The name to which I refer was Woodhatch. Instinctively I translated it as Woodpecker. Could this identification be justified? Or was it just a freak of the imagination?

Those who have some acquaintance with the ornithology of Great Britain will recall that there is another British bird, closely allied by the classification of natural orders to the Woodpecker, which passes under the name of Nuthatch. Here we have the same termination as in Woodhatch, and since the bird in question is named from its curious habit of fixing nuts in the bark of trees and similar convenient crevices, and then hammering the shells with its beak, it would seem that the last syllable of its name ought to have something to do with the process of opening the nuts. That is, *Nuthatch* should be cognate to *Nuthack*. We must try and find out whether such a form *nuthack* exists, and if it exists, we must then go on and enquire whether a similar cognate form *Woodhack* can be found to go with *Woodhatch*. Before doing this, a brief justification may be made of the habits of the Nuthatch in getting at its food. White, in his *History of Selborne*[1], remarks of the Nuthatch that

> As this artist has no paws to hold the nut firm while he pierces it, like an adroit workman he fixes it, as it were, in a vice, in some cleft of a tree or in some crevice; when, standing over it, he perforates the stubborn shell. We have often placed nuts in the chink of a gate-post where nut-hatches have been known to haunt, and have always found that those birds have readily penetrated them. While at work they make a rapping noise that can be heard at a considerable distance.

The description makes it easy to see that the Nuthatch belongs to the same natural order as the Woodpecker.

Now let us see what Sir Thomas Browne says of the Nuthatch. In discussing certain birds found in Norfolk, he remarks as follows[2]

> Picus Martius, or Woodspeck, many kinds, (including) a dun-coloured little bird, called a nuthack. They make holes in the trees without any consideration of the winds or quarters, butt as the rottenness thereof affordeth convenience.

Here we see that Sir Thomas Browne has rightly recognised the Nuthatch as belonging to the same order as the Woodpecker; but he tells us further that the birds in question are, in Norfolk, called respectively *Nuthack* and *Woodspeck*. Here, then, is the evidence that *-hatch* in *Nuthatch* is the same thing as *-hack*. It is natural, then, to suggest that if we went further north, remembering that *hatch* changes into *hack*, as we pass from South English to North, we might find the Woodpecker under the form *Woodhack*. Enquiry elicits the interesting information that the Woodpecker is actually known as the Woodhack in Lincolnshire. Sir Thomas Browne's other information also turns out to be verified, for the bird is at this very day called in Norfolk the *Woodspack*; and it

---

[1] *Loc. cit.* II. 176.   [2] *Notes on Certain Birds found in Norfolk* in Sir Thomas Browne's works (ed. Sayle), III. 520.

seems clear that we have here (and as we shall see, elsewhere) the equivalent of the German *Specht*. We conclude, then, that the Guildford name which drew our attention is the name of the Woodpecker.

Starting with this discovery we now proceed to the next point, which is that the name in question is not really a personal name at all, but a place-name. For there is, in the same county of Surrey, about two miles from Reigate, a village named *Wood-hatch*: and we naturally infer that the Guildford family are a migration from that particular village, and that their name, as so often occurs in English, is the name of their place of origin. From which it follows that we have discovered in Surrey a Wood-pecker village.

The method of demonstration is very simple, but it has advantages of its own. If we had first found the village, the authorities on place-names, from Skeat downward, would have insisted that Woodhatch merely meant Wood-gate, and that *hatch* was for the Anglo-Saxon *haecca*, a gate. It is chronic with the philologians to explain *hatch* in this way. We are not concerned to deny that their explanation is sometimes correct, as for instance, that in Shakespeare (and in Cambridge Colleges) a buttery-hatch is a half-gate over which beer, etc., can be served; and that a ship's hatchway requires a similar explanation; but if we follow this derivation too closely we shall miss the solution of the corresponding forms in *hack*, for which the same philologians usually refer us to the Norwegian personal name *Haco* or *Hacon*. It is clear that they must be often, perhaps very often, on the wrong track. We propose to them an alternative solution that *hack* and *hatch* are equivalent forms, and belong to the action of the birds referred to in getting their food. In making that statement we open up at once a wide field for further enquiry; for there are a number of places that contain *hack* and *hatch* in composition, and a number of personal names from the same roots. We must clearly go further and see if there are more Woodpeckers on the path before us.

Suppose we go into Hampshire; we shall find a village whose name is *Hatchwood*. Clearly this must be the same name as the Woodhatch with which we started. Then we shall find *Hatch* by itself in Bedford, Surrey, Devon, Somerset and Wilts. In Hampshire we shall find also a place named *Hackwood*, in which the harder northern pronunciation appears somewhat unexpectedly. In Surrey again we find *Hatchlands,* where Hatch can certainly not be a gate, nor can it represent the hacking action of the bird; it must be the bird itself: so that when the personal name *Hack* turns up (as it does in my own family) or the corresponding *Hatch* (as in the case of one of our great Church historians of the last generation), we must say of them that they belong to the Woodpecker clan.

We thus have acquired already a number of Woodpecker centres: nor does it appear that we have done any violence to English philology in drawing the conclusions. The only objection that could be made would be to show that the place-names or the associated personal names which we are discussing are not in their earliest documentary form: every student of place-names knows how the apparent meaning of the name is contradicted, when we come across its archaic form in the Domesday book or the Pipe-rolls. That is the direction in which the traps lie for the unwary amateur. In the present case, however, it is clear that since we have, as has been demonstrated, a village named Woodhatch, and a bird of an equivalent name, the primitive form of the one will be the primitive form of the other, for the same laws of phonetic change may be assumed to have operated in the two cases: hence, whatever the primitive form may be, the place-name and the bird-name can still be identified. We may also say, without making too rapid generalisations, that it will be wise to examine carefully place-names in which *hack* or *hatch* is a factor, in order to see whether they conceal the form or activity of the Woodpecker.

We have also learned another thing from Sir Thomas Browne. His identification of the Norfolk Woodpecker with the Woodspeck opened up at once the connection between the Norfolk name and the German *Specht.* We shall clearly have to collect not merely the English names of the Woodpecker but such names as may correspond to them in French, German or Norwegian, for it is by such identifications that we can make ourselves reasonably sure that our interpretations are correct, and not due to the way-wardness of our own imagination. Suppose we find that in Bavaria the Woodpecker is called *baumhäckel* (baum = tree), the form betrays parallelism with *Woodhatch*; if we had any residual doubt it would disappear on finding that in Prussia the

Woodpecker is called *holzhacker* (holz = wood), which certainly has nothing to do with Anglo-Saxon *haecca*, a gate, and is almost exactly the equivalent of *Woodhack*. The German forms bring out more clearly the meaning of the English: the *hack* or *häckel* is a hoe, the *hacker* is a person who strikes with a hoe or a pick. Either the pick and the hoe have been named after the Woodpecker or conversely. I think we shall see reason to believe that primitive man named his first digging-stick after the bird, and not the bird after his digging-stick. He probably revered the Woodpecker before practising agriculture. There is nothing strange in Picus giving his name to the pick. Let us see what Grimm's German dictionary will say on the points before us. Here is a specimen.

Häckel. Auch der bäume beheckende specht heizt im bair. *baumhäckel* Schmeller 2149 (sonst *baumhacker*): zu diesem häckel stellt sich ganz das mundartliche englische *eckle* a Woodpecker, Halliwell 329 a.

Our journey to the German dictionary sends us back enriched. We are not only told that the *Specht hacks trees*, and so furnishes us with the parallel to our *Woodhack*, but we are told also that there is a nearer parallel to *häckel* in a popular English name for the Woodpecker, which is called in many places *eckle*. If Grimm is right in his parallel, we shall be able presently to explain a number of English place-names. Meanwhile, we note in passing that the Woodpecker is a personal name in Germany as well as with ourselves, and that the author of the *Riddle of the Universe* may at least find out something about himself, whatever he does with the other conundrum. Here is another specimen from Grimm, which will give us some information in another direction.

baumhäckel, *picus arborarius, weil der specht in den baum hackt, baum-bicker,* östr. *baumhackel* Höfer 1. 66.
der baumheckel, der baumheckel
kaum auch hernach gelaufen
Uhland 36.
grünspecht und baumhäckel, den bienenstocken böse gäste: Hohberg 2. 376. vgl. bienenwolf und specht.

This entry is peculiarly interesting: the Woodpecker *hacks* at the tree, he is called also *baumbicker* which is a very close parallel to *woodpecker*, and stands for an original *baum-picker*. Then we have the dialect form, *baumheckel,* and lastly a reminder that Germany also had a Beowulf, or Bee-wolf, which was an enemy to the beehives, just as we saw in the case of King Keleos.

We have before us the task of collecting the folk-names of the
Woodpecker, and the corresponding names in European languages,
more or less closely related to our own. For the former we may
naturally refer to Wright's *Dialect Dictionary*, where we shall find
a good many collected, or to Swainson's list in *Folk-Names of
British Birds*: for the latter, we shall use an important article
by Riegler in *Zeitschrift für Volkskunde* for 1913 (heft 3, pp. 265–
277), as well as a special Scandinavian list, kindly furnished to
us by Dr Feilberg. To take an example: Wright will tell us that
in Shropshire, the Woodpecker is known by the name of *Yockle*.
A reference to a county map will show us, at a short distance from
Shrewsbury, a village named *Yockleton*. If *Yockle* is really the
Salopian Woodpecker, then *Yockleton* is a Woodpecker village;
and this result is practically independent of the original form of
the place-name; for setting aside the possible influence upon the
life-history of a word from the addition of a suffix and consequent
change of accent, we must admit that whatever Yockleton goes
back into, Yockle will go back with it. That means that we have
discovered another Woodpecker village; perhaps it may even be
the twin-village attached to Shrewsbury[1].

Here is another curious place-identification. In Yorkshire
the Woodpecker has had a number of popular names, such as
Yaffle, Speight and *Pickatree*. The first is supposed to represent
the laughing cry of the bird (one of its two fundamental notes),
the second we shall establish presently and show that it is the
German *Specht*; the third is the name that perplexed me most,
as I could not find an analogical formation, nor a corresponding
place-name. For this reason I stated in *Boanerges* (p. 332) that
I had not found any parallel to it. *Pickatree* may be interpreted
as *Pick-on-tree*, that is, it may be explained by the action or the
position of the bird. The parallel form comes to us from Denmark,
where we find the name *Traepikker* for the Woodpecker, or the

---

[1] The students of place-names are all at sea over Yockleton, which is in the
Domesday Book in the form Loclehuile (or Yockle-hill). Johnston, in his
Place-Names of England and Wales, reports the matter as follows: "*Yockleton,*
(Shrewsbury) *Dom.* Loclehuile, error for Geochulle, just as *Dom.* has Locheshale
for Yoxall. This seems to be 'village of the *yokel,*' at least there seems no likely
man's name; only *yokel,* 'a boor, a country lout,' is, so far as records go, a recent
and dialect word, for which we can find nothing earlier than Jamieson's *yochel,*
'a big stupid person.' Probably it is derived from *yoke* and meant originally 'a
ploughman.'" See also Duignan, *Staffordshire Place-Names,* pp. 177, 178.

Norwegian *Traepikka*; and I see now that *Picktree* is the name of a village in Durham not far from Chester-le-Street. So here is another Woodpecker village identified.

Woodhack and Traepikker lead us naturally to the discussion of forms which involve Pick, and may be connected either remotely, or directly through the Romance languages, with the name of the Woodpecker. There seems to be little doubt that the Woodpecker is directly responsible for the personal name *Peckover,* either through the Italian *Pico verde* (Green Woodpecker) or the equivalent French *Pic-vert*; and when we find in Cheshire a village named *Pickforton*[1], it seems almost a necessity to explain it as the town of the *Pic-vert*. What then shall we say of Picton and a number of associated forms? It used to be said that *Pickshill* in Bedfordshire was named after the Picts: as Skeat points out it is "absurdly spelt *Pictshill* in the Ordnance map." Skeat's explanation is that the "prefix is the A.S. *Pices,* gen. of *Pic,* answering to the modern E. *Pika* as a surname[2]." Very good, but who is *Pic?* A closely connected form is *Pickhill* near Thirsk in Yorkshire, of which Johnston notes that in the Domesday Book it is *Picala, -ale* and that it means the *Nook of Picc.* Who then is *Picc?* (See what Skeat says above in reference to the Suffolk name Spexhall.)

When we come to discuss Pickton and Pickworth, we are advised that in A.D. 1340 Pickton (Cheshire) is spelt Pykton, and that Pickworth (Rutland) is in A.D. 818 Piccingawurth and in A.D. 1460 Pykeworth. So that these names represent the "town of *Picc*" and the "farm of the descendants of *Picc.*" Who then is *Picc* who gives his name to so many centres in different parts of the country? Searle's *Onomasticon* suggests as Saxon names both *Pic* and *Picc,* but has only a single instance of either. It is

---

[1] I am not quite satisfied about *Picforton*; in the Domesday Book it is given as Pievreton, which looks like an attempt to render the French *Pie-vert* or *pic-vert*. On the other hand, in documents as early as 1093 A.D., and for centuries after, the common spelling is *Pecforton,* the second *e* of the Domesday name being replaced by an *o*: it is possible that this stands for Pic-ford-ton, which brings the Woodpecker in by another road. See what is said below on *Pickford* as a Woodpecker name.

[2] So Wyld and Hirst, *Place-Names of Lancashire,* p. 209, identify *Pexhill* as follows:

1296 ⎱
1305 ⎰ Pexhille: De Lac. comp. pp. 45, 48, 59.

The "hill" named after a person called *Paecc,* or *Pecc.*

clear that the personal name must have existed, but how does it colour the country-side so widely? The simple and natural explanation is that the Woodpecker has been a factor in personal and local names, just as he gave us Picus and Picenum in ancient Italy.

In this particular case the name has reached us by two roads. It may be the Latin *Picus* through French influence. It may, however, have come from the north of Europe, and answer to a Scandinavian *Pikker*. In this connection here is an important piece of evidence showing that the Woodpecker was actually worshipped on the Baltic as late as the seventeenth century. The evidence comes to us from John Gutslaff, who took down the subjoined prayer from the lips of an old Esthonian farmer. (John Gutslaff is the man to whom we owe the design, in A.D. 1656, of translating the New Testament into the Esthonian dialect, which translation, according to Darlow and Moule, was published at Riga in 1686[1].) The prayer is quoted from Gutslaff in Grimm, *Teutonic Mythology*, and apparently from Grimm by Frazer (*G. B.* II. 368), and Fiona Macleod in the *Turn of the Year*, pp. 48 *sqq.* I make these references as it is important to see how Grimm has been treated in citation. Now for the prayer, as it is given in the English translation of Grimm.

Dear Thunder (Woda Picker), we offer to thee an ox that hath two horns and four cloven hoofs, and we would pray thee for our ploughing and sowing, that our straw be copper-red, our grain be golden-yellow. Push elsewhither all the thick black clouds, over great fens, high forests and wildernesses. But unto us ploughers and sowers give a fruitful season and sweet rain. Holy *Thunder* (pöka Picken) guard our seed-field that it bear good straw below, good ears above, and good grain within.

Upon this Grimm remarks that *Picker* and *Picken* are closely related to the Finnic *pitkäinen*—thunder, and that "as the fertility of the land depends on thunder-storms and rains, Pickäine and Zeus appear as the oldest divinity of agricultural nations." Apparently Grimm had not the least suspicion that the Pikker whom he was identifying with the Thunder was the Woodpecker. Frazer is in the same case, for in transcribing Grimm, apparently

---

[1] Gutslaff's book is called *Kurzer bericht und unterricht von der falsch heilig genandten bäche in Liefland Wöhhanda.* Dorpt, 1644.

See also Petersen, *Finn. Mythol.* p. 17; Rosenplanter's *Beiträge*, heft 5, p. 157.

from the original, he gives us "Dear Thunder...holy Thunder," and thus drops Pikker altogether.

Fiona Macleod, however, who is normally far less trustworthy, as scholars would judge, has given the right meaning to the passage in a delightful essay on *The Awakener of the Forests*, where he quotes Grimm as follows:

Perhaps to this day the Esthonian peasant offers in his heart a prayer to *Pikker, the Woodpecker-god, god of Thunder, and storm-god too,* of the glades and fields where these can devastate—a prayer such as that which Johann Gutslaff, a Finnish author of the seventeenth century, cites as the supplication of an old Esthonian farmer: Beloved Pikker, etc.

No doubt this is the correct explanation, the Esthonian cloud-compelling Zeus was the Woodpecker. If he is called Pikker or Pikken, we need not detach these from the Scandinavian forms in which he appears as *traepikker* or *traepikka,* nor from the parallel forms in English dialects: and when a statement of English names traces back a form to a Saxon *Picc* or *Picca,* we ought to have no hesitation as to the meaning of the name: it is our primeval god that has come upon the scene!

The question then takes the form of an enquiry into the distribution of the "pick" sites. We must collect the probable names, and endeavour by means of early documents, Anglo-Saxon charters, Domesday entries and the like, to find the earliest forms in which the names appear. Sometimes names which have provoked suspicion will have to be removed from our collections; but sometimes it will be found that, where no suspicion had been provoked, the early documents will betray the form. Here are some names that will repay examination:

Pickford (Warwick).	Pickhill (N. Riding of Yorks.).
Pickmere (Cheshire).	Pickwell (Sussex and Leicester).
Pickwick (Wilts.).	Pickness (Yorks.).

Some of these are surely Woodpecker names.

Then we can also employ the parallelism of the forms which occur under "hack" and then under "pick." It must be lawful to group together

Pickness (Yorks.) with Hackness (Yorks.).
Pickford (Warwick) with Hackford (Norfolk).
Pickwood (Yorks.) with Hackwood (Hampshire).
Picton (Yorks., etc., etc.) with Hackton (Essex).

If one of a pair is a Woodpecker name, the other will almost certainly follow the classification.

When we examine the distribution of the places identified we see that they are all over the country-side, so that it will not be permissible to assume that they are personal names in the first instances, or generally. A clan of Picks, Pikes or Peakes, would not be spread over the country: we might trace their migrations, or even determine their nationality, but even then they will only lie on lines and in defined districts. The Woodpecker, however, cannot be "cribbed, cabined or confined" by boundaries other than forests; and at first the forests are everywhere. The personal names, however, will have their own interests; sometimes, as we have so often seen, they are place-names obscured: it is interesting to know that the waggons that pass along our roads bearing the name of Pickford[1] owe their superscription to a Woodpecker which once had the duty of guarding the passage of a stream in days when, perhaps, there were no bridges! And of course it is a joy to find the village that Mr Pickwick came from, and to take him back to his place in folk-lore. How he would have loved the study, preferring it even to the tittlebats on Hampstead Heath or to the epigraphic labours of Mr William Stumps!

Our next group is what may be called the Specht-group. Sir Thomas Browne introduces us to it, by the remark that in Norfolk, in his day, the Woodpecker was called *Woodspeck*. This can only be the German *Specht*. Collateral forms will be the Swedish *Hackspett* with the variant form *Hackspik*. The simpler form in that same language is *Spått* or *Spett*. In Norway we have *Spetta* and *Hakkespek*. All these forms are instructive: for instance, the meaning of *Hack* is hardly in doubt; nor need we hesitate if we find in Norfolk the form *Woodspite* to equate the second syllable with *Specht*. In Yorkshire *Speight* is a characteristic name, and it is certainly a Woodpecker. I do not think you will find a single Speight in the whole city of Birmingham, but you will find them abundantly in Yorkshire. The first great Chaucer student bore this name, and he was a Yorkshire man.

Here is a more obscure case. Three miles east of Worcester is a village called Spetchley. The place-namers are in difficulties over its meaning. The matter is analysed by Duignan in his

[1] There is an alternative supposition (v. supra) that, just as *Telford* has been evolved out of a primitive Norman-French *Taille-fer*, which itself subsists among us as *Telfer*, so Pickford may stand for an original *Pic-vert*. But then we have *Hackford* also as a place-name.

excellent book on *Worcestershire Place-Names*. First he collects
the dated early forms: we have

A.D. 816.　Specleaton.
A.D. 967.　Speclea (and so in Domesday).
A.D. 1275.　Spechesleye.

These forms lead to the suggestion of a proper name *spaec-*: but,
says Dr Duignan, there is no such recorded name, nor anything
like it. He then suggests the Anglo-Saxon *spaec*—speech, and
conjectures that Spetchley may have been a place of popular
assembly: but being evidently dissatisfied with his *Garden of
Speech* or *Lea of Speech*, he falls back on the solution "Spaec—
probably represents some unrecorded proper name." He leaves
it unsettled, but his investigation was entirely on the right line.
It only needed the observation that the missing proper name was
(with the smallest internal change) the Woodpecker.

Under this head a number of interesting place-names come
into consideration. The village of Speeton in Yorks, to the north
of Bridlington, is in the Domesday Book under two or three
entries and spellings; there is Specton and Spetton: and which-
ever is the genuine spelling, it must be the equivalent of Speight-
town. We actually get the form *Speighton* in Devon (a county
not very rich in Woodpecker names). We must also examine
Spaxton (Somerset), Spettisbury (Dorset), Speke (Lancashire),
and Spixworth (Norfolk). For the variation between Speight
and Speke we may compare the Swedish forms of the Woodpecker-
name Hackspett and Hackspik. For the meaning of Speke we
have an interesting note in Wyld and Hirst, *Place-Names of
Lancashire*. First the forms are collected:

A.D. 1086.　Spec.
A.D. 1340.　Speck.
A.D. 1509.　Speake.

Then the previous suggestions are canvassed, as to whether it
means "swine-pastures," from the O.E. *spic* which means "bacon":
of which the remark is made that it does not seem probable.
Then comes the suggestion that perhaps it has something to do
with O.E. *sp(r)ecan*, speak, which is dismissed as just as difficult
to believe! Finally, in despair, we are told that "these uncom-
pounded names are very difficult." As may be seen above, the
name could have been found in composition, Specton, etc.

We now come to a very interesting group of place-names,
which are almost certainly connected with a group of folk-names
of the Woodpecker.

It was observed above that Goodall in his *Place-Names of
S.W. Yorkshire* had explained the form *Hickleton* as being a
Woodpecker-ton, because *hicel* or *hicol* is one of the English names
for the Woodpecker. In this he was following Middendorff, who
had apparently learnt from Halliwell that the bird was commonly
called *eckle*. The folk-names come to our aid at this point: for
instance, at the present day the Woodpecker is known all over
Worcestershire as the *stock-eagle* (or *tree-eagle*). Here the *eagle* is
evidently the same thing as the form *eckle* referred to above:
and it will be difficult to dissociate it from *hicel* or *hicol*. In
Northamptonshire, the bird is known by the popular name of
Jack Ickle, which connects itself readily with the other forms.

Now there is a place-name which in one form or other, simply
or in composition, is found all over the country, and it is commonly
supposed that the word *Eccles* means a church and is connected
with *Ecclesia*. That is the popular explanation, and we must
not assume that it is always wrong: there are, however, grave
objections to it. For instance, Mr Horsfall Turner pointed out
that the name was attached to places in Yorkshire where there
has certainly never been a church. In the next place, there is a
simpler form to be detached; and this simpler form *Eccle* cannot
by any subtlety be evolved from *Eccles*. It must be itself the
original, and *Eccles* must be its genitive formation. Not only is
it true of the place-names, but even the associated personal
names preserve the form *Eccle*; I noted it recently in the *Expositor*
in the form *Ekil* (which is the folk-name of the bird in Oxfordshire)
as the writer of an article. Let us see what explanations are
current of *Eccle* and *Eccles*.

Goodall discusses among S.W. Yorkshire place-names the
forms Eccles, Eccleshall, Ecclesfield, Eccleshill, Exley, etc., and
says that "the name *Eccles* in its simplest form" (by which I
suppose he means *Eccles* out of composition) "is to be found as
far north as the Firth of Forth, and as far south as the borders
of the English Channel. There are even instances across the
North Sea. The diffusion can be seen if we register eight cases of
Eccles in Kent, Lancs., Yorks., N.E. Norfolk, Scotch Lowlands,
and N.E. France, together with Ecclesbrook (Worc.), Eccles-

bourne (Sussex, Hants and Derby), Eccleston (Cheshire, two),
Ecclesborough (Berks), Eccleswall (Hereford), Ecclerigg (West-
morland), Ecclesfield (Yorks), Eccleshill (Lancs), Ecclescraig
(Kincardine), Ecclesmachan (Linlithgow) and Ecclefechan (Dum-
fries; the birth-place of Carlyle). Goodall admits that some of
these are genitive formations and is not satisfied with the general
applicability of Ecclesia as an etymology.

It would be certainly difficult to make anything but "little
Eccle" out of Ecclefechan[1], and if Ecclerigg is a correct form, it
carries with it Ecclescraig and Eccleshill. It will be seen that the
Church will have to retire from the ownership of some of the
places[2].

It has been common to refer them all to an Anglo-Saxon
origin; for instance, Duignan, discussing the Warwickshire *Exhall*,
shows that it comes from an eighth century *Eccleshale*, and
explains it to mean *Aecle's meadow-land*, with the remark that
the personal name Aecle is not recorded. Assuming this to be so,
we are at once struck with the fact that the Eccle-names should
apparently be found from the Firth of Forth to the Channel, and
yet no word be found in historical documents of the person involved.
Duignan points out that there is an Anglo-Saxon name *Aegel* or
Aegle, but that this would evolve into *Ayle-*, the intervocalic *g*
becoming a *y*, as in Aylesbury, Aylesthorp, Aylesford, etc.

We have a series of names of the following type:

Aylesbury (Bucks).
Aylesby (Lincs).
Aylesford (Kent) and perhaps as its older name Eaglesford.
Aylsham (Norfolk) with Eaglesham (Renfrew).
Aylton (Hereford) with Eagleton (Hereford).
Egleton (Rutland).
Eggleton (Hereford).
Aylestone (Leicester) and Egglestone (Durham).

The parallel forms seem to confirm Duignan's argument and to
justify the underlying *Aegle*. In that case, it surely must be the
Woodpecker (the *stock-eagle* of Worcestershire): and the question
arises whether *Aecle* is anything else but a duplicate of this, just

[1] *Fechan* is Celtic for "little." Cf. "Llanfairfechan," Little St Mary's.

[2] Mr Moorman, as we stated above, holds to the Church derivation, and will
have Ecclefechan to mean (p. viii) "the little Church," or "the Church of
St Fechin." He has to allow that on his hypothesis of a mutilated Celtic Ecclesia,
such compounds as Ecclestun, Ecclesford, Ecclesfeld are hybrid formations. That
is not exactly fatal, only there are too many of them.

as among the folk-names of the Woodpecker we have (*stock-*) *eagle* and *eckle*. In fact, Eccleshill in Yorks takes the form Eggleshill in the Domesday Book, and Eccleston in Lancs becomes Egleston in the same quarter. We should then understand the wide diffusion of the *eccle*-forms, without any necessary reference to *ecclesia* at all.

Perhaps we may find the two forms in question existing side by side: for example we shall find *Eccles* in Kent in close contiguity to *Aylesford*. We have not, however, yet exhausted the related forms of this group. We have already referred to Middendorff, *Altenglische Flurnamen*, who explains *aeccel, eccel* as the Green Woodpecker, with the modern form *eckle*, and the following Anglo-Saxon instances, *Aeccelcumb, Aeceles beorh*, and *Eccleshall*. Middendorff goes further, and explains the name Hicklesworth (= aet hiceles wyrðe), by equating *hicol* with Woodpecker. If he is right, as he certainly seems to be, we explain not only Hicklesworth, but such forms as Ickleford (Herts), Ickleton (Cambs), Icklesham (Sussex), etc., in all cases without introducing Ecclesia. From not seeing the meaning of the underlying *aecle*, the writers on place-names have got into unnecessary perplexity: Johnston *Place-Names* discusses Eccles as follows:

> *Eccles* (Lancs, Attleborough, Maidstone) and *Ecclesfield* (Sheffield). Lanc. E. *sic. c.* 1100. Sh. E. *Dom.* Eclesfelt, 1179 Ecclesfield. Either L. *ecclesia*, W. *eglwys*, 'a church,' or rare case of a personal name in gen. used for a place, without suffix, '(village of) *Æcel*,' or '*Æcle*,' a known O.E. name....It is hard to be certain which alternative is right; both are contrary to the usual. E.g. why should the name *Æcle* so often be used alone, when almost no other is?

Upon which we remark that it is not absolutely necessary to exclude either alternative, but that, of the two, the Woodpecker generally seems to have the right of way against the Church. Of the names assigned to the Woodpecker, the continental parallels suggest higher antiquity for a form *haeckel*, than for the Worcestershire (*stock-*)*eagle*.

A word may now be added on the form *Fina* (a weak masculine form in Anglo-Saxon) detected by Middendorff and again by Goodall. If this form of the Woodpecker's name be conceded, quite a number of place-names will have to be examined, such as Finborough (Suffolk), Finham (Warwick), Findon (Aberdeen and Sussex), Finedon (Northants), Finstock (Oxford), Finsthwaite (Lancashire), Finsbury (Middlesex). The genitive formation in

Anglo-Saxon ought to be *Finan,* which seems to rule out two or three of our group at once (i.e. if we assume them to be possessive formations). The alternative seems to be the assumption of an O.E. personal name Finn, which can be readily justified. The matter deserves, however, some clearer investigation. Finsthwaite is certainly Scandinavian, as far as its termination goes, and according to Björkman, the name Finn is found in England before the Danish period, but has always a more or less mythological character (whatever that may mean). Can a Scandinavian origin be found for all the forms in the foregoing group?

There is one other perplexing group of names which I have not yet succeeded in resolving, which may have some connection with a hypothetical Woodpecker. I refer to names involving *Clop* or *Clap.* We have in Scandinavia a series of Woodpecker names, such as *Trae-Kloppe* (tree-clapper), *Vidkleppa* (wood-clapper), and in the Rhineland we have the form *Baumklöpper.* There is no doubt that these forms are connected with the German *klöpfen* and the English *clap.* This raises the question whether the Woodpecker may not have had a name of the type *clopper* or *clapper.* The enquiry is the more interesting because of the existence of a number of related place-names which have not yet had their meaning resolved. For instance, Skeat says of *Clophill* in Bedfordshire, that "the sense is uncertain; perhaps it means 'stubby-hill.'" This is not very illuminating. Of *Clapham* in Bedfordshire, he shows that in the parallel case of *Clapham* in Surrey the original form is *Cloppa-ham,* which he says is a genitive plural from *Clop.* But "the meaning of Clop is not certainly known." Duignan suggests a personal name *Cloppa* for *Clopton* near Stratford-on-Avon. *Clopton* would thus be Clopp's town, original form *Cloppantun.* Middendorff suggests that *Clop* is the German *klopf,* and means a rock or boulder. It will be seen that the explanation of the word is much in doubt. It is possible that we may be on the track of another Woodpecker name. I have not, however, yet found the parallel to the German names among the folk-names of the Woodpecker[1]. There are many Claphams, Claptons, and Cloptons up and down the country, waiting for explanation. One *Clapton,* $7\frac{1}{2}$ miles N.W. of Bristol, is called *Clapton in Gordano,* and is said to have abundance of Wood-

---

[1] The Oxford Dict. says that one member of the Woodpecker tribe is called *Clape* in the State of New York.

peckers. We leave this part of the problem for the present unsolved.

From Wright's *Dialect Dictionary* we learn that in Cheshire the Woodpecker goes by the name Ettwall. This is not very easy of explanation; but, whatever it means, we find it as a place-name in the next county (Derbyshire), six miles S.W. of Derby, so that here we recover another Woodpecker site.

Reviewing the investigation of the present chapter it will be admitted that the Woodpecker is in evidence all over the country-side, in the names of places and persons, to a degree beyond what has been suspected, and far beyond what can be affirmed of any other bird. Since there is no reason to suppose that the Woodpeckers outnumbered other birds, singly or collectively, we can only explain the attention given to them historically and geographically by saying that they are the centre of some kind of devotion, and that some, at all events, of the places where we find their names are cult-centres. When personal names contain the Woodpecker element, not derived from previous place-names, it seems reasonable to explain their relationship to the Woodpecker through the same kind of links as in the cases which turn up in Greek and Roman mythology, and to suggest that they stand for some kind of a Thunder-ancestry. In fact, the cult of the Wood-pecker, judged by what we find in the case of Picus-of-Picenum, of Keleos-of-Keleai, or Dryope-of-Amphissa, is probably either a Thunder-cult, or a Twin-cult, or both. We must see if further illustrations can be found of the hypotheses before us[1].

---

[1] Parts of this chapter and the following have been employed in an article in the *Contemporary Review* for Feb. 1916 on *The Place of the Woodpecker in Primitive Religion*, and are reproduced by the permission of the Editors.

CHAPTER III

THE POPULAR NAMES OF THE WOODPECKER

We shall now try to classify roughly the titles and terms by which the Woodpecker is described among European peoples; for, as we have said in the foregoing chapter, it is not reasonable to ignore the Teutonic, Latin, or Scandinavian names which have influenced our own vocabulary. Moreover, since, as we have shown, the country-folk still preserve a number of ancient titles in their local dialects, we have a second road on which to pursue the enquiry, running parallel, or nearly so, to the first. Let us then see whether we can arrange the matter conveniently for study and reference.

Our first group is composed of names which describe the action of the bird in hacking or pecking at the bark of a tree:

Holzhacker (i.e. Woodhacker)	... Germany.
Baumhacker (i.e. Tree-hacker)	... ,,
Baumhäckel	... Bavaria.
Baumhecken	... ,,
Baumbeck	... Tyrol.
Bômhacker	... Rheinland.
Baumpecker	... ,,
Traepikker	... Denmark.
Traepikku	... ,,
Trepikka	... Norway.
Tråknarr	... Sweden.
Woodpecker	... England.
Pick-a-tree	... ,, (Yorks).
Baumklöpper (? Tree-clapper)	... Rheinland.
Trae-kloppe	... Norway.
Vid-kleppe (Vid = wood) ...	... ,,
Ronnenpicker (i.e. Rindenpecker or bark-picker)	Rheinland.
Rine-tabberer	England (Leicester).
Tabberer ⎫ Tapperer and ⎬ ... ... Tapper ⎭	,, ,,

Holtbecker (Holt = Holz = wood)...	Heligoland.
Holzhacker	Prussia.
Tannenbicker (fir-picker)	Switzerland.
Nicker-picker...	England (Notts).
Wood-knacker	,, (Hants).
Woodchuck	,, (Salop).
Woodhack	,, (Lincoln).
Vedknarre (Ved = wood) (The Gt black W.)	Sweden (Dalarne).
Skogsknarr (Skog = forest) ...	,,
Hakel	England (Glouc.).
Hickle	,, (Northants).
,, ...	,, (Warwick).
,, ...	,, (Oxford).
Eccle	,, (Worc.).
Eakle	,, (Glouc.).
,, ...	,, (Oxford).
Hickol...	,, (Hereford).

And a number of related forms :

Hackspik	Sweden.
Hackspett	,,
Hakkespet	Norway.
Stock-hekle	England.
Stock-eakle	,, (Staffs).
Stock-eikle	,, (Worc.).
Stock-eagle	,, ,,
Hickwall	,,
Hickway	,,
Ettwall	,, (Cheshire).
Pic and Pie	France.
Pik'escource (écorce = bark) ...	,,
Picvert (pivert)	,,
Picamaderos	Spain.
Picaposte	,,
Picapotros	,,
Pico	Spain and Italy.
Picchio	Italy.
Ciocanitoare (= knock-with-hammer)	Roumania.
Bocanitoare (= knock-with-beak) ...	,,
Awl-bird	England.
Woodall (Woodwale, etc.)	,,
Cnocell (i.e. pecker)	Wales.
Cnocell-y-coed (i.e. Woodpecker) ...	,,
Coblyn }[1] Coblyn-y-coed }	N. Wales.
Tyllwr-y-coed (= wood-borer)[1] ...	,,

[1] For these two forms cf. Woodall and awl-bird, *supra*.

Hewhole (Prob. hole for holt = holz) England.

Pump-borer	...	...	...	,,	(Salop).
Whetile (prob. = cutter)	...	...	,,	(Essex, Herts).
Woodpie	...	...	...	,,	(Hants, Staffs, Som.).
Taille-bois	...	...	...	France.	
Coupe-bois	...	...	...	,,	
Boque-bois	...	...	...	,,	
Pique-bois	...	...	...	,,	
Perce-bois	...	...	...	,,	
Bec-de-bois	...	...	...	,,	

Then there is a group of names in which the bird's action is compared with various trades and crafts: thus he is called

Zimmermann (= Carpenter)	...	Germany.
Serra-Chiavi (= Key-filer) ...	...	Italy,

and perhaps we should here include

Taille-bois (= Carpenter) as above   France.

His physical peculiarities are answerable for

Longo lengo (= long tongue)	...	Provence.
Braga rossa (= red hose) ...	...	Italy.
Culo rosso (= red rump) ...	...	,,
Beretta rossa (= red cap) ...	...	,,

From its supposed diet of wood or of bees, it is called

Woodsucker ...	...	...	...	England (New Forest).
Holtfraeter (i.e. Holtfresser or wood-				N. Germany.
eater)				
Xylophagos ...	...	...	...	Mod. Greek.
Beo-wulf (= Bee-wolf)[1]	...	...	Anglo-Saxon.
Bienenwulfe (= Bee-wolf) ...	...	N. Germany.

The next group to study is the Specht-group. The meaning of the ground-form is still uncertain: we have the following names in current use:

Specht[2]	...	...	...	Germany.
Spette ...	...	...	...	Denmark.
Sortspaette (Gt Black W.)...	...	,,		
Grônspaette (= Green W.)...	...	,,		
Gråspaette (Spotted W.) ...	...	,,		

[1] The name is due to a misunderstanding of the Woodpecker's diet: a similar mistake prevails to-day with regard to the Honey-buzzard, which eats the larvae of the bees and wasps. Grimm points out that this supposed hostility between Woodpecker and Bee is the reason why people who carry about with them the bill of a Woodpecker are never stung by bees.

[2] The name appears modified in Spessart (=Spehteshart =Spechtwald).

Flagspaette (= flecked or spotted W.) Denmark (Jutland)
Flakspaette ... ...   ,,   (,,)
Flakstaer (= Spotted tail?)   ...   ,,   (,,)
Spått *or* Spett   ... ...   Sweden.
Grönspett   ... ...   ,,
Grönspik   ... ...   ,,
Hackspett (ut sup.)... ... ...   ,,
Hackspik   ... ...   ,,
Spetta... ... ...   Norway.
Hakkespek   ... ...   ,,
Gronspetta (= Green W.) ... ...   ,,
Speight   ... ...   England.
Woodspite   ... ...   ,,   (Norfolk).
Woodspeck   ... ...   ,,   (,,).
Woodspack   ... ...   ,,   (,, , Suffolk).
Sprite (? *for* Spite)... ... ... ,,   (Suffolk).
Espeche   ... ...   Old French.
Speht ... ...   Old High German.
Speh ... ...   Elsass and Rheinland.
Grünspek (= Green Woodpecker)...   Tyrol.
Spaetr... ... ...   Old Norse.
Kakspjöt[1] ... ...   Norway.

We come now to folk-names derived from the note of the bird.
It has two cries, one which has been compared to the neighing
of a horse, and to the human laugh: the other when it is supposed
to be calling for rain. Thus it has been called

Waldpferd (= Woodhorse) ...   ... Germany.
Boschhengst (= Thicket-horse) ...   ,,
Baumreiter (= Tree-rider) ... ...   ,,
Baumrutscher (= Tree-creeper) ... Egerland.
Wieherspecht (= Neighing W.)   ... Tyrol.
Laughing-bird   ... ... England (Salop).
Laughing Betsy   ... ...   ,,

and perhaps to the same group belong

Yaffle ... ... England (Yorks, Surrey,
                                    Hants).
Yaffler... ... ... England (Hants).
Yaffingale   ... ...   ,,
Yelpingale   ... ...   ,,
Yockle   ... ... ,,   (Salop).
Hufil ... ... ,,   (E. Riding of Yorks).

[1] I am not clear that this is a Specht-form nor as to its meaning.

The rain-cry is variously represented and gives rise to the following names:

Giessvogel (= pouring-rain-bird)	...	Germany.
Gissvogel	...	Austria.
Giitvogel ⎫ Gietvogel ⎬	...	Low German.
Gütfügel ⎭		

The cry of *geuss, geuss, giet* (= pour) is said to augur a down-pour of rain. We have the same belief in the power of the Woodpecker's cry to produce rain in the popular language of the West of England. In Devonshire the farm-labourers say, "Us be goin' to have rain; the 'oodalls are hollering" (i.e. the Woodwalls, or Woodwales, are crying). Another form arising out of the rain-cry, and belonging to the same imitative sound-names as Giet and Giess, is

Ki-ek　　...　　...　　Mongolia.

This is evidently a parallel name to Giet. It occurs in a curious Mongol story[1] to the effect that the Woodpecker was once a servant of the prophet Moses, and very much given to thieving. At last Moses lost his temper with him, and punished him by making him live on nothing but wood. The Woodpecker tries to say, 'There is nothing to eat,' but he only gets as far as kē-ek, and no one can understand him. Here we have the rain-cry but with a new explanation and a fresh mythology. This name interests me, because Kiek (dissyllable) is the mysterious and hitherto unexplained name of a friend of mine (formerly Congregational minister at Hanley, and now at Halifax). His name gave me much perplexity, but I see now that he is a Woodpecker crying for rain.

In Germany, also, we find the closely-related *Giek* and the name of *Holzgieker*. At least these appear to belong to the same group. In France, also, there is a popular name *Plieu*, expressing at once the sound of the bird's cry and the expected rain: thus Michelet says[2] that "In dry seasons especially his lot is wretched; his ‚prey flies from him and retires to an extreme distance, in search of moisture. Therefore he invokes the rain with constant cries of *Plieu, Plieu*." These rain-making functions are of the highest importance in the study of the Woodpecker-cult; for

---

[1] Quoted in Dannhardt, *Natursagen* 3, 2327 from *Folk-lore Journal* 3328.

[2] *The Bird* (Eng. Trans. p. 225).

they descend from a time when the Woodpecker was the Thunder-bird, and are to be studied in the light of the bird's ancestry. To this rain-group belong the following:

Regen-vogel (= Rain-bird)	Tyrol.
Rainbird } Rainfowl }	England.
Rainpic (= Rain-Woodpecker) ...	,,
Rågnfågel (= Rain-bird)	Sweden (Stockholm).
Rågnpytta	,, (Finveden).
Regnkråke (= Rain-crow)	,,
Pic de la pluie (= Rain-Woodpecker)	France.
Avocat de Meunier (= Miller's Coun- sellor)[1]	,,
Windracker	Altmark,

and then there is a triad of English names:

Storm-cock and } Weather-cock }	England.
and Weather-hatcher	England (Sussex).

These last should be noticed because they show that the weather-cock on the church spire is not necessarily a cock and does not by its mobility indicate weather that is likely to be, by pointing out from which quarter the wind is coming. The bird was originally fixed in position and not rotating; he was actually the weather in his own person; originally in a prophylactic sense of Thunder averting Thunder, and then as a rain-producer, because Thunder brings rain[2].

There are a few other names which may be attached to this group, where the Woodpecker is perhaps named after other birds, such as:

Waldhalm (= Forest cock) ...	Germany.
Holzgüggel (= Wood-cock) ...	Switzerland.
Hohlkrähe (= Wood-crow) ...	Switzerland.
Holkraaka (= Wood-crow) ...	S. Norway[3].
Spelkrôka, etc.	Sweden.

[1] Because if there is no rain there will be no grain. We shall refer to this later.

[2] The cry of the bird for rain is said in Shropshire to be *weet, weet*, as the following bit of dialect, reported by Margaret Burne (of Newport) in *Folk-Lore* for 1911 (p. 238), will show: "I've allus noticed that when the Ayquils hollohs 'weet, weet,' we gets rine. If you listen to them you can hear them speak quite plain 'wet, wet.' They've been holloling very loud this last day or two, and see what rine we've got. They hollohs as they flies along." Note the dialect variation of *Ayquil* for *Eckle*.

[3] Thus they say in dialect in S. Norway, "Holkraaka spaar regn," i.e. the Hole Crow predicts rain.

Then there is a group of playful names: from its Latin form of Picus Martius we have three French names:

Grande Marte	... ...	France (Isère).
Little Martha...	... ...	,, (,,).
St Martin's Bird	... ...	,, (,,),

to which add

Maréchal Ferrant	... ...	France,

and the Gertrude group from Scandinavia:

Gjerstruet	... ...	Norway.
Gjertrusfugl ...	... ...	,,
Gjertrudsfugl ...	... ...	Sweden.

The foregoing names are interesting, because they are religious as well as playful. The substitution of Martha for Mars is very like what goes on when a divinity is turned into a saint in the Calendar: for Picus Martius is not a modern classifier's name, it appears for example, as Piquier Martier (genitive?), in the Iguvine tables[1].

As for Gertrude, she is probably a direct substitute for Freya, and we shall perhaps be able to show that Freya has a peculiar position in the cycle of rain and thunder deities.

In North Italy the Woodpecker is named:

Catlinoun ...	... ...	Lombardy.
Great Catarina	... ...	Cremona,

while in England it passes under the humorous title of "Laughing Betsy" or "Jack Ickle" (i.e. Jack Woodpecker), (Northants); the form Ickel may be classed as above with Ekil, Hickle, etc. In Denmark it has the name "John Larssen" or "Lassen." The surname is common enough and perhaps is destitute of any special meaning.

Nearly all the foregoing names belong to the Green Woodpecker (*Gecinus viridis*); the Great Black Woodpecker (*Picus Martius*) is not an English bird. Occasionally the names refer to the Great Spotted Woodpecker or the Lesser Spotted Woodpecker; and some names are especially given to the two latter species. Thus the Great Spotted Woodpecker is, in the south of England, known as the *French Galley Bird*; and the Lesser Spotted Woodpecker is in Sussex called the French Magpie, or *French Pie*. The latter is sometimes known as the Small Barred Woodpecker from its black and white stripes.

---

[1] See Bücheler, *Umbrica*, p. 37.

In Cornwall the green Woodpecker is called "Kazek," a name which is, at present, unexplained. In Shropshire another name is "High-hoe," which is also obscure.

The following groups of names are of some importance, on account of their antiquity:

Witwoll	...	...	...	...	England.	
Witwall	...	...	...	...	,,	
Witwale	...	...	...	...	,,	
Woodwall (perhaps the same as Woodawl, *supra*)					,,	(Somerset, Devon).
Yokel ...	...	...	...	...	England.	
Yukel ...	...	...	...	...	,,	
Yuckel	...	...	...	...	,,	(Wilts).
Yockle	...	...	...	...	,,	(Salop).

The Woodwall or Woodwale is a very early English form. It occurs in the English *Romance of the Rose* in Thynne's edition of 1582 as follows:

> For there was many a byrde syngyng,
> Throughout the yerde al thringing,
> In many places was nightyngales,
> Alpes[1], finches, and *woodwales*,
> That in the swete song delighten.   (l. 653.)

> And he was al with byrdes wrien,
> With popingay, with nightingale,
> With cholaunder and with *wodewale*,
> With finche, with larkes and with archangell.   (l. 902.)

We have now collected nearly 170 Woodpecker names, of which the greater part are English; and it must be clear that there was a special interest in the bird and that it also discharged useful functions. If we can be clear upon this point, then the step to identifying the Woodpecker centres as cult-centres will not be a difficult one to take.

[1] i.e. Bullfinches.

CHAPTER IV

THE WOODPECKER AS RAIN-MAKER

A very little study of the foregoing list of Woodpecker names will show that it is *par excellence* the Rain-bird. Quite a number of its names turn upon the discharge of the functions of rain-making. In this respect it differs from another closely associated cult-bird, the Robin Redbreast. Both of them are original Thunder-birds, but while the Robin is still connected with the Thunder, and in some quarters is the original Fire-bringer, the Woodpecker has largely moved from Fire in the direction of Water. Sometimes, as in the Esthonian prayer quoted in a previous chapter, he is invoked to keep hurtful thunder off and to bestow sweet rain. His function is undergoing differentiation. As the Thunder, he, or his cognate, the Domestic Cock, will protect buildings, but this is automatic and needs no ritual. He can stay outside the Church and keep the Thunder off: when rain is wanted he must come inside and we must talk to him.

If we examine the French Woodpecker names we see (1) that we are to ask for rain; (2) that what we are really asking for is bread. The bird is the *Miller's adviser*; as pointed out above, no rain means no grain. If there is no rain the Woodpecker must be scolded, as all fetishes, for not giving bread. This is perfectly simple, but it is surprising how much light it throws on certain folk-traditions. Take for instance, the story of old Mother Red-cap who was turned into a Woodpecker. Why was she metamorphosed? The answer is that Jesus came to her door when she was baking and begged a bit of bread. When she finally refused to give him the bit of dough which had expanded in the oven into a great cake, she is cursed for not giving bread, and sent up the chimney and becomes *Gertrude's fowl*. What she really refused was rain, and she was really a Woodpecker, just as King Picus, or King Keleos, or Zeus before he was Olympianised. Why is she called Gertrude? The answer is that Gertrude is the Christian substitute for Freya. Was Freya, then, a rain-maker? Let us look into the matter and see.

There seems to have been a division of function between Thor and Freya in the matter of meteorology. Thor is certainly the Thunderer, the Scandinavian Zeus, and must be related to a previously existing and worshipped bird-form. It does not, however, appear that Thor is appealed to for rain. Thus Grimm says (I. 175):

> I cannot call to mind a single passage, even in O.N. legend, where Thorr is said to have bestowed *rain* when it was *asked* for: we are only told that he sends stormy weather when he is angry.

So there is nothing exactly answering to Zeus. Let us see what they say of Freya: we are to show (i) that she is the cult ancestress of Gertrude; (ii) that she has to do with rain. As regards Gertrude, the identification was suspected by Grimm, from the custom of drinking the *minne* of St Gertrude the first night after a decease.

> Freya's dwelling is called *Folkvangr* or *Folkvangar*, the plains on which the (dead?) folk troop together; this imparts new credibility to the connection of St Gertrude, whose *minne* is drunk, with Frowa, for the souls of the departed were *supposed to lodge with Gertrude the first night*. (Grimm, I. 305.)
>
> It was customary to honour an absent or deceased one by making mention of him at the assembly or the banquet and draining a goblet to his memory; this goblet, this draught, is called in O.N....*minne*. (*Ibid.* I. 59.)
>
> In the Middle Ages it was two saints in particular that had *minne* drunk in honour of them, John the Evangelist and *Gertrude*....
>
> In a MS. of the 15th century we are informed:
>
> Aliqui dicunt, quod quando anima egressa est, tunc prima nocte pernoctabit cum beata *Gerdrude*, secunda nocte cum archangelis, sed tertia nocte vadit sicut diffinitum est de ea. (*Ibid.* I. 61.)

So Grimm suggests that Gertrude discharged Freya's functions to the dead.

Is Freya a rain-goddess? The answer is that she is a weeping goddess, and that mythology is invoked to say why she weeps. She has been forsaken by her husband, and wanders round the world seeking him and shedding tears. Freya's tears are said to be golden, gold is named after them, and she herself is said to be "gratfagr," i.e. fair in greeting (i.e. weeping). (See *Snorre* 37, 119, 113.) Freya is, then, easily identified as a rain-goddess:

that is, then, the reason why the old Mother Red-cap, who becomes a Woodpecker, is called Gertrude, and why the Woodpecker is, in Scandinavia, called Gertrude's fowl.

There is a variant form of the Gertrude story in English folk-lore, which Shakespeare has immortalised in Hamlet. Ophelia is made to say, "*The owl was a baker's daughter*: Lord, we know what we are, but we know not what we may be." Here the old lady who was baking is replaced by a masculine baker, whose daughter refuses bread and is turned into an owl as a punishment. We have had occasion to point out elsewhere that the owl is one of the denizens of the sacred (hollow) tree, and is an unsuccessful Thunder-bird. It shows its hostility to the Robin, for example, and when the poor little bird has its feathers burnt off in bringing fire to mankind, and the other birds take up a feather collection for its benefit, the owl is the only bird that refused to put anything in the plate!

This Scandinavian legend is really the story of the bird that gave no rain. In studying it in its Norse form, we shall find commonly a second folk-tale attached to it. The old woman strikes Christ on the head, so as to produce a putrefying wound, out of which bees arise. It is easy to detach this part of the story and study it separately, as it occurs in the folk-lore of eastern Europe. The two legends lie near together, for, as we have shown, and will explain more at length, the origin of bees and bee-culture is in the same tree that houses the Woodpecker. When we have briefly examined into this new element in the lore of the bee, we can return to the Woodpecker and discuss some further points in his cult.

CHAPTER V

THE WOODPECKER AS *DUX VIAE*

It has been shown, in the examination of the function of the Heavenly Twins, that they were in request, *inter alia*, as Rainmakers on account of their kinship with the Thunder-god, and so were the patrons of fertility; and it was further explained that the Twins were the guardians of travellers by sea and land, and in particular presided over dangerous situations on seas and rivers, and that they became ultimately the patrons of navigation. In a previous chapter we showed that the same rain-making art is credited to the Woodpecker in northern Europe and probably elsewhere in extreme antiquity. This does not in the least surprise us either in the case of the Twins or of the Woodpecker, for the Twins are the children of the Thunder and the Woodpecker is the Thunder. We are now going to show that Woodpecker-cult is like Twin-cult in its patronage of the traveller and the sailor, and we shall express this briefly by saying that the Woodpecker is *Dux Viae*.

Let us, for a moment, recall the methods by which we established the care of the Twins over the traveller. One way was to notice the saints in the Christian calendar who have displaced the Twins, and who occupy themselves with the guardianship of dangerous places on rivers, or dangerous passages in the seas. For example, Cosmas and Damian had charge of the rapids on the Cañon of the Upper Euphrates, where their ruined temple still stands. Lower down the river, at Zeugma, where the road to the east crossed the river, they are said to have had a sanctuary which was restored by one of the pious emperors. These two cases constitute guardianship of the river-rapids and guardianship of the river-fords (or at least of the traject). On the Bosporus, where we have shown[1] the Heavenly Twins to have been the Pilots and

---

[1] *Vide infra* p. 66.

Wardens of men sailing to or from the Euxine, we find them replaced by St Michael the Archangel on both sides of the Strait, and the substituted cult continues to the present day. Now let us see whether there is anything parallel to this in English life. We have our own peculiar dangers both in sea-faring and in land-faring. At sea we shall find our coasts marked by sanctuaries only one degree removed from original Twin-cult, shrines of St Cosmas and St Damian, St Crispin and St Crispian, St Michael the Archangel and the like. Especial dangers, like the Goodwin Sands, are covered by special patronage, as the history of Kent Churches will abundantly show. When we move inland we find that there are no great rivers with rapids to be negotiated like the Euphrates; the traveller's difficulty in early English life is the ford; there are no bridges, or next to none. Hence the traveller is in danger from the depth of the stream and from the nature of the bottom. If he is observant he will name the ford and describe its character. When the bridge comes it will naturally appear where there was formerly a ford or perhaps a ferry. Then the name of the place will be Stamford Bridge, i.e. Stainford Bridge, or Ferry Bridge. The name will tell the nature of the original stone crossing and the primitive method of transit. Here is a little statement on the matter from Moorman's *W. Riding Place-Names* (p. iv).

Let us for a moment consider...the name Bradford. Bradford is now a city with a population of nearly a quarter of a million; but it is by no means certain that when it received·its name—the broad ford—there was a single house there. Like Aberford, Woodlesford, Milford, Garforth, Horsforth, etc., it is a landmark name, denoting the spot where a stream, together with the swampy land adjoining it, was crossed by a ford. It is probable that the name Bradford was bestowed, at a time when bridges were little known, upon scores of fords in all parts of England.

This extract shows us clearly the importance of the ford in topography, and the fords are the danger-points to the traveller: he may be

Drowned in passing through the ford
Or killed in falling from his horse.

Here then he will need protection and direction. These will be the places in which to look for saints, or for the Twins and the Woodpecker who preceded the saints, and are the cause of the saints. So we may begin by asking whether the topography of

Great Britain betrays any sign of the presence of the Woodpecker at the fords.

Looking back over the pages of the foregoing enquiry into the Woodpecker-names of Great Britain, we see at once that we have Pickford and Hackford, and Aylesford, and Eaglesford, Ickleford and Ecclesford. The probability is that most of these are cases where the ford was marked by the supposed presence of a Woodpecker. It could not mean that one person saw a Woodpecker at a particular river-crossing and made the fact permanent by the name: he could not secure that the bird, if observed, would stay. Nor is it a case like Oxford, or Horsford, where the prefix tells us something about the depth of the passage. The natural explanation is that the Woodpecker is there as the patron of the passage; and if the danger of the crossing is real, I should not be in the least surprised to find that the nearest Church had a dedication to or a shrine of a Twin-cult. That is a matter worth enquiring into on its own account: for even if we had no Woodpecker names, the places where the ancient roads cross the rivers are the danger-points; there, if anywhere, we should expect twin-oversight, or the like. Perhaps this will come out clearer to the future student of the topography of the British Isles.

Assuming that we have cases of fords presided over by the Woodpecker, can we say anything on the larger theme of the Woodpecker as *Dux Viae*? In the Kalevala the Woodpecker is the special guide of the huntsman. He is appealed to under the name of Nyyrikki as follows:

> Nyyrikki, O Son of Tapio,
> Thou the mighty red-capped hero,
> Blaze the path across the country,
> And erect me wooden guide-posts,
> That I trace this evil pathway,
> And pursue the righteous roadway,
> While I seek my destined quarry.
>
> (Kalevala: tr. Kirby, XIV. 37.)

Here the Woodpecker is entreated to score the trees on the track of the huntsman, so that he may not lose his way.

The same kind of guidance by a Woodpecker appears to be implied in a passage from the *Lay of Igor* (79) of which Grimm remarks[1] that "Woodpeckers by their tapping show the way to

---

[1] *Mythol.* (Eng. tr.): ii. 675.

the river." Does this mean that they are to see the traveller across? At all events, the bird is the *Dux Viae*.

It is quite likely that the recognition of guidance by the Woodpecker may underlie the tradition of the people of Picenum, that they were guided to that city by the bird after whom the city is named.

There seems, too, some reason to believe that the Woodpecker is a patron of travellers by land and water, just as the Dioscuri are. ·

CHAPTER VI

THE ORIGIN OF BEES

We have shown that primitive man made the right attribution of the invention of honey one of his scientific enquiries, and came to the conviction that the discovery of this valuable adjunct to civilised life in his day was due either to Aristaeus, who is a by-form of Zeus, or to the Kuretes, the fosterers of the infant Zeus, and that Aristaeus was connected with the Hollow Oak, and the Kuretes with the Woodpecker. There is, however, another question which provoked the enquiry of our ancestors; they appear to have studied the problem of the origin of the bee as well as that of the discovery of honey. To this enquiry there seem to have been various solutions; one of them is well known to scholars, viz. that bees arise spontaneously in the carcase of an ox which has been left to decompose, or actually buried with the exception only of its horns. There is a well-known Biblical parallel in the story of the bees that took possession of the carcase of a lion which had been slain by Samson. The references to these ox-born swarms will be found in Robert Tornow's book at sufficient length, and need not here be repeated. It seems, however, to be clear that the observation of the early natural philosopher had gone further: he did not, indeed, understand that the hive of bees was ruled by a queen; from Aristotle onwards, and probably long before the time of that particular philosopher, it was supposed to be a king, but he did understand that the larvae in the hive were young bees, and this set him thinking on two lines: first he compared the larvae with the maggots and worms of a decomposing body, and asked himself from what body they had come. Next he asked himself the question as to why the little bees were so white, and the mature bees so black. European folk-lore contains interesting and instructive cases of these enquiries, from the study of which we shall get some valuable information as to the thought processes of the early and nascent scientific mind.

In the first place, it was natural that a comparison should be made between the little bee-larvae and the maggots of decomposition. *Quite possibly this may be the idea which lay at the back of the story about the finding of bees in the carcase of a dead or buried ox.* A very small confirmation of theory by experiment, such as the actual finding of bees or honeycombs in the skin of such an animal, would lead to the belief that the bees had sprung in some way from the decomposed animal. Experimental confirmation, however, is not strongly insisted on in primitive science.

Here, however, a fresh difficulty would arise in the case of the finding of the bees and their combs and larvae in the oak-tree. Where was the decomposed or decomposing animal in such a case? What creature furnished the worm that was the larva and became the bee? That is one of the questions to which we and our ancestors have to find the answer.

The other question relates to the difference in appearance between the larva and the bee. Why did the white become black? Who or what blackened it? And in the same connection, who is responsible for the fact that the bee is almost cut in two centrally? Let us see what the European peasants say on this point to-day. One story is that the larvae came from a wound in Christ's forehead, it having been noticed that the requisite putrefaction could occur in living bodies as well as in dead bodies. If we ask how Christ came to have a wound in his forehead, the answer was easy: we have already drawn attention to the Norse legend of how the old woman (Mother Red-cap, let us call her, in Norwegian her name is Gertrude) who refused bread to Christ was changed into a Woodpecker, or Gertrude's fowl, and flew up the chimney. The story teller goes on to say that she had actually struck Christ on the forehead with the baking shovel or the kitchen poker. This wound in his head produces worms, which, when placed in a hole of a tree, become a swarm of bees.

The story of the Norse Mother Red-cap appears in many forms. We have shown in the previous chapter that Shakespeare has one such form in mind, when he makes Ophelia say in Hamlet,

> They say the owl was a baker's daughter,

in which we have the same underlying theme of an ungracious baking-woman, who would not give bread to the hungry, and was changed, as a punishment, into an owl. The story is told of

Christ, or of Christ and Peter: but it is probable that this is only a Christianisation of an earlier folk-tale. The variation between owl and Woodpecker is one that we have already come across traces of. There are other translations in folk-tales of the ungracious baker's wife or baker's daughter, who puts the bit of dough a-baking for Jesus, and then refuses it to him because it has swelled to too great a size. Sometimes she becomes a peewit, sometimes a tortoise. The meaning of these variations is not always clear. Occasionally, there is no resulting metamorphosis. For instance, among the Basques it is the Virgin who begs bread from an old woman; the bit of dough grows to a great loaf in the usual manner; the old woman is not transformed, but a curse is laid on the village for ever and ever[1].

It is to this theme that the story of the bees that spring from the wound in Christ's head has been attached. This latter story is not really a part of the Red-cap legend: it has been attached to it by means of the introduced baking-shovel or kitchen poker. We can see this by watching the variants of the latter part of the story.

Among the Tshuvasses in Bulgaria it is said that the bees crept out of the navel of the great God, Mun Jurě, instead of out of the forehead of Christ[2]. The Russian peasants say a similar thing, by making the origin of the emerging bee (or larva) the navel of Christ on the Cross.

The bee-worm is taken from a hole in the Divine body and placed in a hole in the tree. It is easy to see that we have here the tree in which the bees live, artificially duplicated: we have both the anthropomorph and the tree-form or phytomorph. Christ comes in as being himself the Thunder-man, or the Son of Thunder; he is, therefore, animistically identified with the sacred Thunder-tree; and the bees, which are found in the holes of the trees, belong to his body: they come from a hole in his head, when the bees' nest is high up, and from his navel when the bees' nest was, as Hesiod says, in the midmost bark.

One of the simplest forms, completely independent of Mother Red-cap, is told in German Bohemia. Jesus and Peter were going through a forest, and came to a hollow tree. "What is the use

---

[1] The series of uncharitable bakers can be studied in Dannhardt, *Natursagen*, II. 123 *sqq.*

[2] Strauss, *Die Bulgaren*, p. 12. Dannhardt, *loc. cit.* I. 128.

of this hollow tree?" said Peter. Jesus, whose forehead was itching, drew Peter's attention to it. A maggot came out, which Jesus set in the hollow tree. Later on, when they passed that way again, the tree had become a beehive[1].

We have now detached and explained the primitive conception of the origin of bee-life, and can see the underlying theme. We may now go on with some further early speculations which have come down to us in the folk-lore of eastern Europe.

It is apparent that, to our ancestors, the reason why the bee has turned black is due to the fact that someone (the Devil by preference) has struck it with his whip. For instance, the Wallachian peasants say that the bee used to perch on the Devil's head and overhear his plans and designs as he talked of himself. Then he would fly away and tell God what the Devil was doing. This enraged the Devil, so that one day he struck the bee with his whip, and made him turn black. He also cut him clean in two, or nearly so.

In another form of the legend, it is St Peter who struck at the bee; but this variant is not idle or useless, for the narrators say that Peter struck the bee with his *fiery lightning whip*[2]. Here the suggestion is made that the whip which has struck the bee is the lightning; the Devil being, as in so many cases, the disguise of the Thunder. The consequences of this suggestion, which can be carried into very early times, are so important that we purpose to treat them in a separate chapter. For the present we note that the bee has been thunder-struck.

Now let us return to the story of Mother Red-cap, and of the owl who was a baker's daughter. We can understand the variation between Owl and Woodpecker, as explained above: they are rival Thunder-birds, with a common liking for hollow trees, and there is a feud between them in consequence of their claims to Thunder rank. The Owl is well known in folk-lore as being the enemy of the Woodpecker; it is not so generally known that it is hostile to another Thunder-bird, which does not live in a hollow tree, the Robin Redbreast. When the Robin burnt his feathers in bringing fire to men, and all the other birds were, out of gratitude or sympathy, lending of their plumage, the owl

---

[1] Dannhardt, *loc. cit.* II. 131.

[2] Dannhardt, quoting from Albert and Arthur Schott, *Walachische Märchen*, 1845, p. 283 ff.

alone refused to subscribe a feather! The fact is, the owl is an unsuccessful Thunder-god, and he is the victim of jealousy. Other birds have outdistanced him in the discharge of the Fire and Lightning functions[1].

Now when we try to explain the two metamorphoses before us, the Mother Red-cap into a Woodpecker, and the Baker's Daughter into an Owl, we shall easily see that the key to the situation is that somewhere there has been a failure to discharge a function. We have the theme underlying all the legends, she gives no bread, and this means, she makes no rain, for without rain there can be no bread, either for Christ or Peter or Christ's folk or the poor generally. *Mother Red-cap is the unsuccessful rain-maker.* As to her conversion to bird-form, that only means that she was originally a Woodpecker, like King Picus and King Keleos. Most of these metamorphoses in the story-books took place in the reverse order. We may put it in this way if we please: Mother Red-cap is the primitive priestess and representative of the Woodpecker, and the Woodpecker is the Thunder. So the popular legends as to the failure to give bread (i.e. rain), go on naturally to the punishment of the bird that is responsible for the defect, which suffers from continual thirst, is compelled to drink out of puddles, and whose cry (gi-et, gi-et, ki-ek, ki-ek) is interpreted everywhere to be a call for rain. Thus the whole series of legends is a dramatisation of the failure to bring rain and the proper punishment of such failure[2].

[1] A similar reason underlies the Greek belief in the hostility between the Wren and the Eagle, which appear as rivals for bird-sovereignty (cf. King Picus, etc.). Thus Aristotle speaks of τρόχιλος ἀετῷ πολέμιος (*H. A.* 8. 3. 5) and Pliny (*H. N.* x. 74), "Dissident aquila et trochilus, si credimus, quoniam rex appellatur avium."

[2] E.g. in the Teutonic mythology the Woodpecker says "Giet, giet," and is supposed to be crying for rain. Grimm (*Mythol.*, ed. Stallybrass, II. 674), "The green-pecker has the alias *giessvogel*, Austr. *gissvogel, goissvogel*: Low G. *gütvogel, gietvogel, gutfügel*...because his cry of *geuss geuss giet* is said to augur a downpour of rain."

In France he invokes the rain, with constant cry, *Plieu, plieu*, and is accordingly so named. It is easy to see why the bird is called in France *The Miller's Provider*, in view of the equation between rain and bread.

CHAPTER VII

THE LIGHTNING WHIP

Now let us return to the story of the way the Devil struck at the bee with his whip, and the accompanying suggestion that the whip is the lightning. The importance of this suggestion lies in the fact that there are abundant traces of the belief, ranging over wide areas and long tracts of time. For example, Grimm had already noted that the Chinese described the lightning as the whip of the thunder: "For lightning they have along with their regular expressions the metaphorical hū-pien, i.e. *the whip of the thunder* (or *the thunderer*)[1]."

Now it seems likely that this is the direction in which we are to look for the explanation of certain passages in the Rig Veda in which the Açvins and the Maruts (Storm-spirits) are described as carrying a whip. For instance, the Açvins are invited to come and sprinkle the sacrifices with their whip, furnished with sweetness and pleasant of sound. Max Müller's explanation of this prayer was as follows:

As whips had probably some similarity to the instruments used for sprinkling butter on the sacrificial viands, the Aovins are asked to sprinkle the sacrifice with their whip, i.e. to give rain[2].

No doubt rain is one of the services which the Açvins are to render, but it would be difficult to find a more far-fetched and meaningless explanation of their whip.

Myriantheus certainly improved on Max Müller's explanation, by suggesting that the whip was the wind, whose whistling might be compared to the crack of a whip, and which had in it the promise of descending rain[3]. It is, however, much more natural to identify the whip of the Açvins directly with the lightning. This does

[1] Grimm (Jacob), *Über die Namen des Donners*, p. 27, Berlin, 1855.
[2] *Twelve Hymns of the Maruts*, p. 176.
[3] *Die Açvins*, p. 133.

not altogether exclude wind and rain under the similitude of whips; we must not make the definitions of primitive man too precise. In order to establish this point, let us turn to the Atharva Veda, where we shall actually find a hymn addressed to the Whip of the Açvins[1]: from this hymn we propose to make a few extracts.

First we are told (IX. i. 1) that the "Açvins' Honey-whip was born from heaven and earth, from middle air, and from fire and wind."

Again (IX. i. 3): "She (the whip) is the first-born daughter of the Maruts and derives her origin from Wind and Agni " (i.e. Wind and Fire).

Again (IX. i. 10): "The Thunder is thy voice, O Lord of Creatures (sc. Prajapati). A Bull, thou castest on the earth thy vigour. The Honey-whip is the Marut's first-born daughter."

Again (IX. i. 21): "The Whip itself is Heaven, Earth is the handle; the point of juncture is the air's mid-region. *The lash is lightning* and the tip is golden." These passages are sufficient to show that the whip of the Açvins is the Lightning, just as the Devil's whip is the Lightning to the peasants of eastern Europe. We must not equate it with the Wind, for it is the product of Fire and Wind, nor with the Storm-god, for it is the daughter of the Storm; nor must we explain it away in the manner of Max Müller's comments upon the two passages in the Rig Veda where the Whip is mentioned. On the other hand, as we have said, we must not detach the whip too positively from the ideas of Fire and Wind.

The very same hymn in the Atharva Veda brings out clearly the connection between the Twins and Honey. E.g. (IX. i. 16):

As honey bees collect and add fresh honey to their honey-store,
Even so may both the Açvins lay splendour and strength within my soul.

And (IX. i. 19):

May both the Açvins, lords of light, balm me with honey of the bees,
That I may speak among the folk words full of splendour and of strength.

So it seems that the connection between the Twins and the bees, which we had detected in the ancient Greek mythology, as well as the connection between the Twins and the Lightning, can be traced also in the ancient Indian literature and ritual.

[1] Book IX. hymn i.

It is very interesting to see how the folk-lore of the peasants in Wallachia and Russia has led us to the solution of a Vedic riddle which scholars have hitherto failed to resolve.

It is interesting to notice that the Vedic conception of the Lightning as a whip still survives in modern India. Every one has been reading of late Tagore's *Gitanjali*, in which the poetry of Bengal is done into English prose that hardly differs from poetry.

In one of these prose poems God is addressed in the following strain: "Send thy angry storm, dark with death, if it is thy wish, with *lashes of lightning* startle the sky from end to end."

It was natural to imagine that we had here a misprint for *flashes of lightning*; but Tagore informs me, in answer to enquiry, that the text is correctly printed, and that the word has its obvious meaning.

In the Greek mythology the Lightning Whip becomes the special property of Castor the Horse-tamer and Chariot-driver from whom it descends at last to Gervasius of Milan, the patron saint of cab-drivers, and to St Ambrose: in the case of the latter it was exhibited to the faithful in concrete and visible form, as I have shown in the *Cult of the Heavenly Twins*[1]. The Whip is wielded by both the Twin-brethren in the story of Heliodorus in the second book of the Maccabees. They scourged him mercilessly and left him half-dead, using the implements proper to their nobility: and so they preserved the sanctuary at Jerusalem and its treasure inviolate from his touch and greed. That is clearly the way the Twins ought to behave: at an earlier period in history they would probably have struck him directly with Fire from heaven; it would have been the same whip from another point of view.

It is impossible to state the case for the Dioscuric scourging of Heliodorus and his expulsion from the temple, without remembering that there was a somewhat similar case in which the covetous and rapacious traders were expelled from the temple at Jerusalem by a figure wielding a whip of small cords. The suggestion comes from an unexpected quarter that the whip of St Ambrose represents the expulsion of the Arians, as Christ drove the traders from the temple. In the volume entitled

---

[1] *Loc. cit.* pp. 126–128.

Ambrosiana, Prof. Calligaris[1] discusses at length the famous whip of St Ambrose and its history and fortunes, in the course of which he draws attention to the popular belief that Ambrose had scourged the Arians out of the Church in the same way as Jesus Christ had expelled the profane. The illustration is an unfortunate one: for if Ambrose's whip, whether used against Arians or in the defence of Milan and the Milanese, should turn out to be the survival of the Lightning Whip of the Dioscures, which we have been tracing in remote antiquity, what are we to say of the scourge of small cords in the Gospel? Is it another Dioscuric trait in the Gospels, following, in St John's Gospel, the story of the marriage at Cana, for which a Dioscuric affinity has also been suggested[2]? It is not easy to decide the question in the present state of our mythological knowledge. We have proved that Jesus was in certain quarters regarded as a Dioscure, and credited with Dioscuric functions; and we have shown that the story of Heliodorus, which has a certain parallelism with the Cleansing of the Temple, is fundamentally Dioscuric in character. The problem does not seem, as yet, to admit of a complete solution; but we must certainly classify the Temple incident amongst cases of suspected or possible Dioscurism.

---

[1] *Ambrosiana:* where it is the thirteenth essay and occupies sixty-three pages: *Il flagello di Sant' Ambrogio e le leggende delle lotte Ariane.*

[2] The whip does not occur in Mark, whom John is correcting: and it is possible to maintain that it is a later apocryphal addition: by sacrificing the historicity of this detail, it may be possible to get rid of the Dioscuric colour in the cleansing of the temple.

CHAPTER VIII

CAIN AND ABEL

I am often asked by those who are interested in Dioscurism on the side of the Christian Scriptures, whether the case of Cain and Abel at the beginning of the Book of Genesis is not a story of origins Dioscurically told. It has always seemed to me, however, to be best to defer the discussion of doubtful cases of Biblical Dioscurism, and to concentrate one's critical attention on those which are reasonably certain, on which we have a *prima facie* probability, and then to proceed to the more doubtful cases in the light of the results thus obtained. For this reason we put the story of Cain and Abel on one side in the first survey, for the account does not say that they are twins, and if they are not twins they have to be inferred to be such by the Dioscuric elements in their experience, which is something like building a structure and putting in the foundations afterwards. It is not really as illogical as that: the inference as to twinship may be perfectly lawful, even if no definite statement on the point is forthcoming: in that case the other observed Dioscuric traces are really our foundation: preliminary twinship is not necessary. If, however, we have a case like that of Esau and Jacob, in which twinship is dilated upon by the narrator, it is very easy to go on from this point and identify the Dioscuric features, the fratricidal struggle, the red colour, the dispute as to primogeniture, the exile of a twin in place of his death and the like. No reasonable doubt can arise that the greater part of the story is pure myth.

In the case of the fighting saints in the Maccabees who protect the temple against the rapacious Heliodorus, even though there is no positive statement that they are twins, the parallel stories from Roman History and the like are sufficient to enable us to fill in the omitted detail, and to regard the whole adventure as a Dioscuric incident in Jerusalem's history, as clearly made out as the battle of the Lake Regillus. We cannot, however, at once infer the twinship of Cain and Abel with quite the same confidence of induction. The best way to proceed with the matter will probably be the following.

First of all, as a preliminary observation, note that in the case of the triad, Jabal, Jubal and Tubal in the same chapter (Genesis c. 4), we have a Kabiric group engaged in occupations and the discovery of human arts, just like those which are credited to the sacred twins and triplets of Greece or Phoenicia. Jubal's lyre is the same as Amphion's, or for that matter, Apollo's. Kastor, too, belongs to the same musical academy. Even the parenthetically introduced sister Noema has her parallel in Helen; and although the fortunes of the group are told in an absurdly abbreviated form, the family likeness is not obscured by the brevity of the narration. If you like, it is a Dioscuric or Kabiric snap-shot.

Second, we may say that if we proceed, as elsewhere, by the way of hypothesis, and assign to the hypothesis the value of that which it lawfully explains, then we may test the story of Cain and Abel and see how much of it would be explicable on the hypothesis of twinship. In that case, we note that twinship is not excluded by the narration: all that the book says is that Eve brought forth a man-child, *and said she had gotten Jahveh,* and that she added to bear a second child. If that child is immediately subsequent to the other, then we have a thunder-child and his brother, the typical explanation of twins at one period of human thought. How much would the hypothesis explain of further detail? Obviously the first answer is that it explains the first murder; Cain is equated with Romulus: Abel with Remus or with Kastor. It does, however, more than this: it explains the exile of Cain; for, just as when the twins are tabooed, they are exiled where they are not exposed; so it is perfectly natural that when one twin is killed, the other should be exiled. Thus we see that the real reason for Cain's wanderings does not lie in the fact that he is a proscribed murderer, but that he is a proscribed person who has not been murdered. As he is taboo, a taboo mark is placed on him, probably on his forehead, as it is expressly said to be, for identification.

Thus we explain at once the exile and the taboo. We do more than this, however, for it will be remembered that one of our most important discoveries in the region of Twin-cult was the formation of Twin-towns by the exiled twins and their mother; we have shown that this is the real meaning of the building of Rome by Romulus and Remus, and of a number of other similarly formed towns or sanctuaries. Now in the story of Genesis, it has always been a perplexity of the pious to explain how, when there were, presumably, no more than four persons in the world, or little more than four, one of them should go off into a remote spot and build a city. The inexplicable and sudden advance in civilisation becomes clear as day, when we remark that it is the fashion for twins at an early stage of civilisation to build Twin-towns. The only residual difficulty lies in the fact that the little twin, round whom the twin-town has already developed, is without his mother's care, and has already killed his brother: but this is just the kind of tangle into which mythologists always get: they have to interpret the traditional murder of a single twin, and they say "twin kills twin" and "twin hates twin," and build up explanatory legends. In the story of the building of Rome the same confusion occurs. The mortal twin ought to have died by exposure: he actually goes on till the walls of twin-town are rising, when another story-teller comes forward to explain how Rome was rid of him.

It appears therefore, that the twin-hypothesis is almost a necessity in the Cain and Abel legends; to invoke it is obvious, when we know how the history of ancient peoples is traditionally regarded.

A few words may now be added to show that the direction in which we are throwing our search-light is the real line of advance on the knowledge of Hebrew mythology. By that we mean that, while not denying the existence of Solar myths in the Hebrew and other Semitic traditions, the twin-myths have often the right of way against them. Twin-myths are not really Solar myths, they descend from the thunder, not from the bright sky; and the attempt to read Solar myths on the wide scale into Hebrew history has just the same tragical collapse as it has in the Greek or Roman mythology. For instance, a large part of Goldziher's learned and diffuse *Mythology among the Hebrews* is vitiated by a false starting-point, the universal ubiquitous Solar myth. Let us see, for example, how Goldziher would treat the Cain and Abel story (we might equally have selected the story of Esau and Jacob); here is a specimen[1]:

> The battle of the Day with the Night is still more frequently represented as a *quarrel between brothers*. At the very threshold of the earliest Biblical history we meet a brothers' quarrel of this kind, the source of which is the nature-myth, spread out among all nations of the world without exception. It is not difficult to prove that Cain (Kayin) is a solar figure, and that Abel (Hebhel) is connected with the sky dark with night or clouds....Cain is an agriculturist, Abel a shepherd. We have demonstrated...that agriculture always has a solar character, whereas the shepherd's life is connected with the phenomenon of the cloudy or nightly sky.

It would be more correct to say "we have imagined" than "we have demonstrated." However, to proceed: Goldziher makes some just remarks on the parallelism between Cain (= Smith) and Tubal-Cain, and between Abel and Jabal, some of which is valid, not perhaps etymologically, but because Dioscures and Kabiri are necessarily parallel. He remarks that:

> We have seen above, and I shall show still more clearly...that in the myths of all peoples the Solar heroes are regarded as the founders of city-life, and that a fratricide often precedes the building of the city. The agricultural stage, which is connected with the Solar worship, overcomes the stage of nomadic life, which holds to the dark sky of night or clouds; and, after conquering the herdsmen, the surviving agriculturists build the first city. It will not surprise us if the solution of the question raised by F. Lenormant, "pour en suivre toutes les formes depuis Cain bâtissant la première ville Hanoch après avoir assassiné Abel, jusqu'à Romulus fondant Rome dans le sang de son frère Remus," proves the consistency and universality of the ideas of mankind at the mythic stage in reference to this point. Whether the connection of the zodiacal figure of the Twins with this feature of the myth is so close as this acute French scholar imagines, is an independent question.

Perhaps we have quoted enough to show how completely side-tracked Goldziher was in his investigation of the encumbering solar hypothesis, and how much nearer Lenormant was to the truth than he. Goldziher goes on to explain the wandering of Cain, by the motions of the Sun, who as the hero described in the Psalms, "rejoices to run a race." We cannot run about after him: he is almost as wide of the mark as Max Müller himself! We do not mean to be understood as saying that there are no Solar myths; even the contradiction of them requires correction and modification. Twin-myths, however, are not Solar myths.

[1] p. 110. (My reference is made to the English translation of Goldziher by Russell Martineau.)

We may conclude with the expectation that, like as we have explained mythology in terms of Twins, and have discounted the explanations of many who have preceded us, so there will be those who come after us who will talk of the *Ignis Fatuus* of Twin-speculations, which has led us away from the region of historical truth into that of mythological fancy: for every man walketh in a vain show: he heapeth up hypotheses, and knoweth not who shall annihilate them!

CHAPTER IX[1]

THE DIOSCURI IN BYZANTIUM AND THE NEIGHBOURHOOD

During a recent sojourn in Constantinople, I took the opportunity to verify a hypothesis which I had emitted with regard to the popularity of the Heavenly Twins on the Bosporus, in their capacity of Saviour Gods, and with regard to the influence which that most popular cult had upon the hagiology of the Christian Church. It was not at all surprising that such suggestions of primitive Byzantine worship, and of subsequent Byzantine displacements, should have been made, when one reflects on the extent to which the Dioscures and their alternative Kabirs were in evidence in the N.-E. corner of the Aegean, and all round the Black Sea, from the Symplegades onwards. Was it likely that shrines should be erected to them at Tomi, at Olbia or in Colchis, in Delos or Lemnos or Samothrake or Tenedos, but that the sailors should cease making appeal to them, when passing the Dardanelles, or when working up the Bosporus into the further sea that they so much dreaded? Had Byzantium no blessing in the name of the Twins for those that put out to sea, and no facilities for the emphasis of gratitude on the part of the mariner, who had successfully returned to his port again? And since the care of sailors and the rendering docile of the waves sailed over was only one branch of their saving art, was it likely that the Byzantian colony of ancient days, or the proud city of Constantine, had no memorials of its hero benefactors, and no places where they practised their beneficence? Obviously, it is in the highest degree improbable that the Heavenly Twins had no hold upon the populations that bordered on the Sea of Marmora, or the straits connected with it; and almost as unlikely that there was an

[1] Reprinted from *Essays and Studies* presented to William Ridgeway on his sixtieth birthday, 6 August 1913, by permission of the Syndics of the Cambridge University Press.

abrupt change of faith at the coming of Christianity, which left
the people nothing that corresponded to their original and age-
long devotion to the Great Twin Brethren.

Moreover, there is a reason why the Twins should be in evidence
on the Bosporus, even if they had been altogether unknown in the
Euxine or the Aegean. I have shown elsewhere that the Twins
are always to be looked for in situations of peculiar difficulty or
danger to mariners; that they preside over shallows (as at Cyrene
and Barca over the great Syrtis), over dangerous places (like the
entrance to the harbour at Alexandria or the reef of rocks outside
Jaffa), over all straits, from the English Channel downward, and
wherever a lighthouse or look-out station is to be found (as in
the case of the Pharos at Alexandria or the Dioscureion on Mount
Cassius). The Bosporus, in early times, was marked both by
lighthouses and by look-out stations; it had dangers of its own,
arising from the current which sets through the Strait from the
Black Sea, which is difficult for sailing ships in bad weather, and
for boats propelled by oars in any weather, at least at those points
where the current strikes against some jutting-out headland, or
when the stream is reinforced by the North wind so that boats,
sailing towards the Black Sea, can no more make headway against
it, and have commonly to be carried overland past the points
where the downward stream is strongest.

There is then, on every account, an *à priori* probability that
we shall find the Twins in the harbour of Byzantium and on the
straits; at the Golden Horn, or on the Asiatic or European shores
of that most beautiful of waterways. Now my hypothesis was
that the Twins had been worshipped on the Bosporus at various
points, until they were finally displaced by the Archangel Michael;
and that they discharged naval and medical functions in Byzantium
itself, where they were finally displaced by pairs of Christian
saints, notably by Cosmas and Damian, who had wandered this
way out of Syria and Cilicia.

The first part of the thesis concerned the case of the displacement of the Twins by St Michael the Archangel, in which case it
was necessary to prove that Christian sailors made vows in certain
places to St Michael, and that the Twins had been in those
situations before him. If it can be proved that St Michael received
such worship and had such antecedents, the case is proved for the
Bosporus; and it will be confirmed for every indication that we

may find elsewhere that Michael took over the trade of the Twins, or that he received honours in Dioscuric situations. It was not difficult to make the necessary proofs: Michaelia, in the sense of Dioscureia, are actually in existence, and legends are not wanting which can only be interpreted as meaning that Michael did what the Twins used to do. We will give presently a classical passage which establishes the foregoing statement. I first drew attention to it in c. xvi of the *Cult of the Heavenly Twins*; but as I have had recent opportunity of studying with some care the configuration and currents of the Bosporus, and have also had the opportunity of discussing the whole matter, from the standpoint of Byzantine antiquity, with my learned friend Dr van Millingen, of Robert College, Constantinople, I have been able to improve my former statements and to extend them, so that Dioscurism on the Bosporus can be regarded as finally and sufficiently demonstrated.

We will arrange the argument in the following order:

(i) There are special points of danger on the Bosporus.

(ii) At some of these points shrines of St Michael still exist.

(iii) There are also a number of look-out stations and signalling stations, and lighthouses which appear to be of venerable antiquity.

(iv) There is literary evidence that the Michaelia on the Bosporus were originally Dioscureia.

In order to make these points clear we must take the Bosporus steamer, or its equivalent, a Murray's *Handbook* for travellers. When we have thus discussed the topography and the steniography (if I may coin a word), we can return to Constantinople and take up the similar problems which that city presents of the transition from popular Dioscurism to equally popular Christian hagiology. This transition is easier than it looks. Strange as it may at first sound, the Dioscuri are not felt to be a cult alien to monotheism. This is true both for Palestine and for Constantinople; it is true even for Rome. A man was not the less a good monotheist Jew, because he believed that Jahweh had come with the Dioscuri to converse and banquet with Abraham at the Holy Oak in Mamre. If he had any theistic qualms, he silenced them by rechristening the angels of the visit as Michael and Gabriel; but any unprejudiced person can see that it is a Theophany accompanied by a Dioscurophany, and it is probably quite a late alteration to dress the Twin Brethren as archangels. It would be easy to show that Dioscurism was current in Jerusalem to within a hundred years of the Christian era, and the cult resumed its rights when the Christian era had arrived, so soon as the Fall of the City had announced the cessation of the more highly evolved national ritual. Near Constantinople, Dioscurism held its own under the Christian regime without suspicion; Constantine decorated his new city with the ancient statues of the Twins, although he founded the city as a monument of the victory of Christianity over Paganism!

Now let us return to the Bosporus, and make our Periplus, or more exactly, our Anaplus and Cataplus of the various stations. The first point of danger that we reach is at Arnaût-Keui, where the current, which has been running down the Asiatic shore in great force, sets across the strait to a point just above the beforementioned village. Now let us see what Murray says of our voyage:

ARNAÛT-KEUI, *Albania village*, is the ancient *Hestiae* or *Anaplus*, which was later called *Vicus Michaelicus*, from the celebrated church of the archangel Michael which was built there by Constantine the Great and repaired by Justinian. The Church was destroyed by Sultan Mohammed II, and the material was used in the construction of the castle at Rumili-Hissar....It is built on the S. side of AKINDI BURNU, *current cape*, where the current runs so strong, four knots an hour, that small vessels and kaiks generally land their crews and track round the point. Trackers, *yedikjis*, can always be obtained on payment of half piastre each. In stormy weather the passage round is dangerous for kaiks, and the current here is called SHEITAN AKINDISI, *Devil's current*.

Here, then, we have our first Michaelion; it is clearly due to the danger of the navigation, and this danger was there before St Michael came this way: it is, therefore, almost certain that sailors had a shrine, in early times, in the neighbourhood of Arnaût-Keui.

The historical details in the foregoing passage can be verified from Sozomen (*H. E.* II. 3); he definitely says that the place was called Michaelion for a primitive Hestiae. The place was on the right hand as you came down the strait from the Black Sea; it was about 30 stadia from the city, as the crow flies, or more exactly as the mariner crosses the bay, but it was more than 70 stadia, if you coasted round the bay and did not cut across. The detail about the restoration of the Michaelion is due to Procopius, who says that there were shrines of St Michael, both at Hestiae and on the opposite side[1]. According to him

---

[1] Procopius, *De aedific.* I. 8, 9.

there was a point, clearly a promontory, called Proöchthoi by the old men, where on the European side was the Anaplus, where sailors worked up stream, and where the shrine of St Michael stood. There was another Michael shrine on the opposite side, and a third at a place called Mōkadion, which has yet to be identified, where Justinian restored the buildings. The evidence for Michaelia is increasing.

Continuing our journey towards the Black Sea, and passing Bebek and Rumeli-Hissar, where Darius crossed and Mahmoud II, and where the great American college now stands, we come to a place called Stenia, or the straits. It is a wooded shore, enclosing the best harbour on the Bosporus, the scene of many sea-fights, and of much ship-building. Here the Argonaut tradition is in evidence. The Argonauts had landed on the opposite shore, where Amykus the King of the Bebryces ruled, at the foot of the Giant's Mountain. Apparently Amykus regarded the straits as his own, and the adjacent wood and water. Whatever the Argonauts got, either in right of water-way or in right of water-supply, they had to fight for: and the story of their victory over the pugilistic Amykus at the hands of the equally pugilistic Pollux (Polydeuces) is a favourite theme with the great Greek poets: the story is splendidly told by Apollonius Rhodius and by Theokritus, and was probably frequently put on the stage. According to Murray's *Handbook*, the place where the Argonauts took refuge, when first threatened by Amykus, now known as Stenia, was originally called Leosthenius and Sosthenius.

It bore among the Byzantines the names of *Leosthenius* and *Sosthenius*. The first name is derived from its founder, Leosthenes the Megarian; the second, from the temple of safety, Sosthenia, erected by the Argonauts, out of gratitude for their deliverance: ...in memory of their victory they dedicated the temple (Sosthenia) with the statue of the heavenly face. Constantine the Great, who found here the temple and the statue of a winged genius, converted the former into a church; and the winged genius, who appeared as a saviour to the Argonauts, into the archangel Michael, as the commander of its heavenly host.

Here is Michael again in evidence, and in connection with an Argonaut temple. It is clear that there must be some reason for his constant appearance, beyond the occurrence of a particular statue at the special point. Michael is a Byzantine cult, and must be regarded as replacing an earlier cult. Moreover, in the story which we have just been reciting, the whole of the legend has not

been told: for it will appear that the popular belief related that
Michael was the very person who fought with Amykus: in other
words, *Michael at this point was Pollux.* The verification of this
lies in what may be called the classical passage for the change of
cult from the Dioscuri to Michael, a statement by John Malalas[1],
from which the previous account was taken, to the following
effect:

Malalas begins with the story of how the Argonauts, working
up the Hellespont, were attacked by the Cyzicenes, whom they
routed in a naval combat; after having slain Cyzicus, the king
of the city, and captured the place, they found, to the mutual
regret of themselves and the Cyzicenes, that they were in tribal
fellowship: so they built an expiatory shrine and consulted the
oracle of Apollo, as to its dedication. At this point the chronographer makes the god prophesy the coming of the Virgin Mary
and her Son, an oracle which the Argonauts inscribe on their new
building, which they somewhat inconsistently consecrate to the
Mother of the gods. This only means that an early temple of
Rhea or Cybele has become a Church of the Blessed Virgin, and
Malalas proceeds to state this definitely: καλέσαντες τὸν οἶκον
Ῥέας μητρὸς θεῶν, ὅστις οἶκος μετὰ χρόνους πολλοὺς ἐγένετο
ἐκκλησία τῆς ἁγίας καὶ θεοτόκου Μαρίας ὑπὸ Ζήνωνος βασίλεως.
It is interesting to notice how the chronographer has projected
back the later consecration on the earlier so as practically to make
the Argonauts responsible for the whole. The story then continues, that the Argonauts made for the Princes' Islands, and then
passing Chalcedon, they attempted the passage to the Pontic Sea
(Malalas says, ἀνῆλθον τὸν Χαλκηδόνος πλοῦν, περᾶσαι βουλόμενος
τὸν ἀναπλοῦν τῆς Ποντικῆς θαλάσσης: we should correct περᾶσαι
to πειρᾶσαι, they were for *trying* the passage to the Euxine).

In this attempt they were set upon by Amykus. They fled
in fear to a wooded bay (evidently the bay of Stenia), and here
there appeared to them a vision of a fearsome man with wings,
who made them the oracular promise of a victory over Amykus.
In commemoration of which victory, they erected a shrine and a
monument of the Power that had appeared to them, calling the
shrine or the place Sosthenes, because of the salvation from their
enemy. It was this shrine that Constantine came to see, and
remarking that the memorial appeared to be half-angel and half-

---

[1] Malalas, *Chron.* IV. p. 78.

monk (ἀγγέλου σημεῖον σχήματι μοναχοῦ), he prayed for further
information as to the Power in question; he incubated at the
shrine, and in a vision of the night it was disclosed to him that it
was a memorial shrine of Michael: ἐκπλαγεὶς ἐπὶ τῷ τόπῳ καὶ
τῷ κτίσματι, καὶ εὐξάμενος γνῶναι ποίας ἐστὶ δυνάμεως ἀγγέλου
τὸ ἐκτύπωμα, παρεκοιμήθη τῷ τόπῳ καὶ ἀκούσας ἐν ὁράματι τὸ
ὄνομα τῆς δυνάμεως, εὐθέως ἐγερθεὶς ἐκόσμησε τὸν τόπον, ποιήσας
κατ᾽ ἀνατολὰς εὐχήν· καὶ ἐπωνόμασε τὸ εὐκτήριον, ἤτοι τὸν τόπον,
τοῦ ἁγίου ἀρχαγγέλου Μιχαήλ.

Here again we see Malalas projecting Christian matter back
on the displaced shrine, just as he did with the dedication of the
shrine at Cyzicus to the mother of the gods. What is certain
from the story is that a shrine has been converted to Christian
uses, which formerly was connected with the Argonauts, and with
the fight over Amykus. The displaced occupant of the Heroon in
question is not the winged genius that promises the victory, but
the quite unmonastic and scarcely angelic person who secured
the triumph; in other words, either Pollux, or the Dioscuri in
common. According to this the converted shrine is either a
Dioscureion or a Jasoneion, the two terms for sailors being very
nearly equivalent. Michael may, therefore, be regarded as a
displacement of a Heavenly Twin, Pollux by preference.

We come now to the entrance to the Bosporus: at this point
we have the invasion of another cult from the Black Sea, that of
Serapis. There are Serapeia as well as Michaelia and Dioscureia.
We come on such a Serapeion, near the mouth of the Chrysorrhoas,
and here Murray's *Handbook* reminds us, "Jason, after having
offered sacrifices on the Asiatic shore to the twelve great gods,
erected an altar to Cybele." So we are once more on the track
of the Argonauts, in whose company Castor and Pollux find a
place. Here, too, we find the ancient Pharos, and a custom-house
for each side of the strait. If we may treat the modern names as
perpetuating ancient sanctities, we have two sacred trees, one on
each shore, giving their names to *Rumili Kavak*, the European
poplar, and *Anatoli Kavak*, the Asiatic poplar. The lighthouse
and look-out station stood at the head of the ravine, and, according
to Murray, bore anciently the name of Ovid's Tower, or the
Turris Timaea.

This was the old Pharos, from which torches were held up at night, whose
lights, placed in a straight line with those at the mouth of the Bosporus,

saved the ships navigating the Black Sea from being wrecked on the Cyanean rocks or the Thracian coast.

At Anatoli Kavak, there was again a temple, said to be dedicated by Jason to the Twelve Gods, on his return from Kolchis. This Hieron is now occupied by the Genoese castle at the entrance to the Black Sea; but it had been formerly taken over by Justinian, who built here a church and dedicated it to the " Archangel Michael, leader of the Heavenly Hosts, who was the special guardian of the straits of the Bosporus." Note how Michael appears to be following the track of Jason. He is clearly an Argonaut in disguise!

As we return down the strait on the Asiatic side, we shall presently come to Vani-Keui, then to a large Barrack, and the village of Kulehli or Kuleh Bagcheh. Here again we shall find a church dedicated to St Michael. The guide-book informs us that:

> Formerly the church of the Archangel Michael stood here, exactly opposite to the one built on the European side at Kuru Chesmeh. The Archangel Michael was regarded as the special guardian of the Bosporus, and hence churches were dedicated to him at Anaplus, Hieron, Kuru Chesmeh, and Kuleh Bagcheh.

I am not quite sure whether the Michaelion at Kuru Chesmeh is distinct from the one at the Anaplus. It seems to be the same as the one previously described.

We noted above that we passed the village of Vani-Keui. At this point the hill above the village has a fine range of landscape, and is admirably suited for a look-out station. It is actually employed to-day for wireless telegraphy, and in Abdul Hamid's time was one of the fire-stations of the city. It stands to reason, however, that in the ancient time when there were no telegraphs, and when one could not always be sure of crossing the strait, a fire-station for Constantinople would never be placed on the Asiatic shore. Moreover, there is a high tower in Stamboul to-day that expressly serves for a fire-station, from which to announce conflagrations.

The stations at Vani-Keui may be taken for an original look-out station, with a possible Pharos, and in that capacity both it, and the corresponding fire-station in Stamboul, were probably Dioscureia.

We have now followed St Michael up and down the Bosporus. We find him on both sides of the strait, presiding over sanctuaries which appear to occur in pairs. These sanctuaries appear to be either Jasoneia or Dioscureia. The story in Malalas appears to identify Michael with Pollux the Argonaut, rather than with Castor or Jason. Serapis, whom Leucius suggests as the ancestor of Michael, is clearly not to be thought of.

It will be interesting to see how far this connection between Michael and the Twins can be made out elsewhere. There is one curious case which came to my notice in recent years; the newspapers reported that at the great eruption of Vesuvius, the stream of lava and mud from the crater had overwhelmed the church of St Michael, which was formerly a shrine of the Heavenly Twins[1]. No doubt there are many more such cases besides the one I accidentally stumbled upon.

Now let us return to harbour and see what traces we can find archaeologically of the Cult of the Twins. We have already suggested the possibility of the existence of an ancient look-out station on the highest part of Stamboul.

We learn from Zosimus[2] that when Constantine began to plan his new city, he found the statues of the Dioscuri on the place where he was planning the new Hippodrome. He did not remove them. It is even said that he went further, and brought from Mt Dindymus a statue of Cybele, which was credited to the Argonauts. So Constantine had not quite accomplished his religious revolution! Probably, as the Sea of Marmora would have been visible in those days from the Hippodrome, the place was a look-out station, and a Pharos, which the carefully preserved statues of the Twins help us to recognise as a Dioscureion.

There was another shrine of the Twins at the head of the Golden Horn, on the hill above Eyoub. Hesychius Milesius is quoted by Ducange in *Constantinopolis Christiana*, lib. I, p. 15, to the following effect[3]: τῶν δὲ Διοσκούρων, Κάστορος δὲ, φημὶ,

[1] The information came in a Reuter telegram; and I noted it in *The Western Daily Mercury* (Plymouth) for Ap. 10, 1906. The despatch concludes as follows: "The road between Cercola and Ottaiano is destroyed. It is covered with burning mud. Refugees from the district of Ottaiano state that eight or ten houses and five churches have collapsed, among them being the Church of San Michele, which was rich in artistic treasures and was built on the site of the ancient Castor and Pollux Temple."

[2] II. 30, 31.

[3] Hesychius Milesius 4, 3. The goddess Semestra here mentioned was a nymph or nereïd, whose cult preceded the arrival of the Greek colonists: she belongs to an old nature worship.

καὶ Πολυδεύκους, ἐν τῷ τῆς Σεμέστρας βώμῳ, καὶ τῇ τῶν ποταμῶν μίξει, ἐν ᾧ καὶ λύσις τῶν παθῶν τοῖς ἀνθρώποις ἐγένετο.   Aedem Castoris et Pollucis aedificavit idem Byzas ad Borbyzae et Cydari confluentes; ad Semestrae aram et fluminum confluentes, ubi et a morbis homines sanabantur.

The streams above mentioned are what are now popularly called the "Sweet Waters of Europe"; and the site of the Temple of Castor and Pollux here given corresponds, with sufficient nearness, to the site of the Church of Ss Cosmas and Damian, on the hill above Eyoub.

It is interesting to notice that the Twins appear at the point in question as healers, and it is as healers that the famous fee-less doctors, Cosmas and Damian, displace them. Another tradition, preserved by Dionysius of Byzantium, connects the sanctuary at the Sweet Waters of Europe with Jason and his companions, which is a slight variation from the preceding: according to Dionysius, Barbyses, after whom one of the streams is named, was either the person who reared Byzas, the founder of Byzantium, or he was the steersman of Jason and the Minyans.   The alternative is to describe the sanctuary as a Jasoneion or a Dioscureion, a choice which will frequently occur[1].

Justinian, who professed to have been healed by the Cosmas and Damian Twins, built churches in their honour, not only in Constantinople, but also in Cyrrhus, near the Euphrates, where their bodies were supposed to be lying[2], and at Aegae, and perhaps at Zeugma on the Euphrates, where they had charge of the passage of the river.   That they commonly displaced the pair Castor and Pollux is betrayed by a naïve story, told by their hagiographers, of the discomfiture of some unbelieving, or ill-believing Greeks, who attempted an incubation in the new Church (or old Temple), and were reproved by the saints who told them, "You seem to imagine that we are Castor and Pollux; we beg to inform you that we are Cosmas and Damian!"   Thus were the wicked Greeks reproved for imagining that it was the original firm, who were doing business at the old stand, under a new name.

The saints in question, whom we unhesitatingly identify as

[1] Dion. Byzant. *Anaplus*, ed. Wescher, p. 11, ἄρχεται δὲ τῶν ποταμῶν Κύδαρος μὲν ἀπὸ θερινῆς δύσεως, Βαρβύσης δὲ ἐπὶ θάτερα κατὰ βορέαν ἄνεμον. τοῦτον οἱ μὲν τρόφεα καλοῦσι Βύζαντος· οἱ δὲ Ἰάσονι, καὶ τοῖς σὺν αὐτῷ Μινύαις ἡγεμόνα τοῦ πλοῦ· τίνες δὲ ἐπιχώριον ἥρωα.

[2] Procopius, *De aedif.* II 11.

Dioscures, not only because they were twins, but because they discharged twin-functions, became the centre of a Greek brotherhood, and gave their name to an open space in Constantinople, known by the name of Cosmidion. When they moved West and took their place in Old Rome, they arrived by two roads; one of which led them near to the Forum to found the church of Ss Cosimo and Damiano; the other to the neighbourhood of the Bocca della Verità, a circular drain-head where Romans used to swear, thrusting their hands into the Bocca. At this point was built the church of St Maria in Cosmedin, rebuilt in the eighth century by Hadrian I, with a beautiful campanile. The Church belonged originally to a Greek brotherhood, as is shown by the reference to Cosmedin, and by its alternative title as *Sancta Maria in Schola Graeca.*